Grain of Hope

A MOTHER'S MEMOIR

To Lisa,
May hope be a lantern unto your feet.

Dolores Pratt Chandler

DOLORES PRATT CHANDLER

The Church Online LLC, Publishing Division
Pittsburgh, PA

DEDICATION

"Though he slay me, yet will I trust in him..."
-Job 13:15 KJV

This book is dedicated to my daughter, Sonja, who as a little girl peered through the windows of her parents' lives, helplessly watching as they were immersed in the illnesses of her baby brothers. As an innocent child, Sonja, you were too young to know or understand why you would become a great sacrifice and later a savior.

May God continue to bless your life and fill any empty place in your heart with His love.

Grain of Hope: A Mother's Memoir
by Dolores Pratt Chandler
www.doloresprattchandler.com

© 2016, by Dolores Pratt Chandler All rights reserved.

Published by The Church Online, LLC
Visit our website at www.thechurchonline.com
Printed in the United States of America
First Printing: December 2016

No part of this book shall be reproduced, stored in a retrieval system, or transmitted by any means, electronic, mechanical, photo copying, recording, or otherwise, without written permission from the publisher. No patent liability is assumed with respect to the use of the information contained herein. Although every precaution has been taken in the preparation of this book, the publisher and author assume no responsibility for errors or omissions. Neither is any liability assumed for damages resulting from the use of information contained herein.

For information, address the publisher:
The Church Online, LLC
1000 Ardmore Blvd.
Pittsburgh, PA 15221

International Standard Book Number: 978-1-940786-44-5

Library of Congress Catalogue Card Number: Available Upon Request

THE HOLY BIBLE, NEW INTERNATIONAL VERSION®, NIV® Copyright © 1973, 1978, 1984, 2011 by Biblica, Inc.® Used by permission. All rights reserved worldwide.

Printed in the United States of America

Trademarks

All terms mentioned in this book that are known to be or are suspected of being trademarks or service marks have been appropriately capitalized. Use of a term in this book should not be regarded as affecting the validity of any trademark or service mark.

Some names have been changed.

Published by The Church Online, LLC

TABLE OF CONTENTS

Introduction 11

PART 1
The Journey 19
Sonja 31
Glenn 37
Tyrone 63
Life-Threatening Surgeries 69
Suicide vs. Salvation 83
A Day at the Park 91
Starting Again 97
Moving On and Away 101
Patrick 107

PART 2
Growing Our Family 113
Metamorphosis: From Caterpillar to Butterfly 117
Bright Beginnings 127
School and Work Bound 131
Ebbs and Flows 137
Friends, Family, and Fun Times 141
A Shattered Dream 151

PART 3
A Special Type of Grief 165
A Beautiful Tribute 171
Life, Death, and Finding an Acceptable Peace ... 173
Sonja: A Reflection on my Daughter 177
Moving On: Jacky and Me 185
Activating the Power of Hope 195

About The Author 201

INTRODUCTION

Grain of Hope is a heartfelt memoir written to inspire and kindle hope in anyone suffering in silence and believing that there is no light at the end of the tunnel. It is a personal account of a significant part of my life where without hope, I really don't believe I would have lived to write this. It is a story about the ever-evolving personal relationship I have with God, unveiling an intimacy of faith, love, and hope between a fragile young mother and her Creator.

I began writing this book in 1988. It has always been extremely difficult and heart-wrenching to express my feelings openly. I guess I wanted to avoid thinking about what happened to me, and I really didn't want to relive the past. I also felt uncomfortable revealing a very intimate part of my life with strangers. Therefore, I put it off for many years. Unbeknownst to me at the time, this book was meant for today.

As it turns out, it has been very therapeutic to relive the past and express my life's journey during the time of my sons' difficult lives. I encourage all grievers to release some of their burden by pouring out that awful sorrow privately on paper. It was both cleansing and freeing for me. More importantly, I believe it gives a voice to others who have been suffering in silence. I am hopeful that my story will give meaning and hope to others who waiver on the brink of physical or mental breakdown because of their crisis. *Grain of Hope* will help empower you to pick up the pieces of your broken heart, mend them together again, and allow you to live a wholesome life in the face of any crisis or tragedy. Like you, I once stood on the same shaky ground—distressed, spiritually broken, and emotionally scarred, fighting a battle for lives that I sorely lost. The good news is God was there all the time, connecting His power to the small and fragile hope I was holding onto for dear life. In retrospect, He was everything I needed at times when I thought I had nothing and no reason to live.

Hope empowered me to be a survivor of one of life's most unthinkable crises. The power of hope displaced years of anguish in my heart with a miraculous peace that liberated and helped me to move on with my life. Hope was the bridge to my faith in God and is truly my sense of stability and security. Hope smoothed out the edges of my frayed nerves. It was my equalizer helping to ground me during a struggle. Hope was my spirit reaching out to God, with God extending his hand to me and imparting

INTRODUCTION

faith. Faith reassures me that the Almighty has the power and ability to change any circumstance, or change me to overcome the circumstance.

So what is hope? Hope is imagining that what you want you will have. Hope is believing that your wildest dream can actually become a reality. Hope is the root cause of taking a chance, being a hero, following a dream, or even writing a book. Hope is the bridge you build to God. God turns that bridge into faith. Faith is the assurance of God's protection and perfect plan for you.

Hope is an instinct that humans use to navigate life. A positive energy and belief that you will receive an acceptable outcome, the word hope rolls off of our tongues easily because it is no stranger to us. A natural response such as intuition, precaution, fear, hunger, thirst, and so on, most people probably never energize the power of hope until they are tested. It resides in your thoughts and its positive effects are manifested by your belief. Hope is used in religions, but religion is not a requirement. Hope partners with any persuasion or philosophy, guiding you through each and every day. A free gift without stipulations or obligations, you can't see hope, touch hope, or taste hope, but it is always there. It is a supernatural expectation deep in your soul assuring you that everything will be all right. Even if the outcome is not precisely what you desired, the answer will give you an acceptable peace.

When we encounter desperate situations, human beings have been known to endure harsh climates, short supplies of food and water, sleepless nights, sickness, disease, and other unpredictable life adversities. When some of us look back on our past, it's a mystery to us how we ever survived. We fought wars, climbed mountains, crossed untamed oceans, risked our lives for another. With all this against us, it takes a profound belief in something to convince us that we will make it to other side. Maybe it's a combination of things we rely on, but I can almost guarantee one of them is hope.

I liken hope to a grain, because a grain is a tiny seed that yields an abundant field of wheat. In comparison, the smallest effort of hope I could muster yielded an abundant supply of sustaining power that I desperately needed during a very crucial time in my life. As it is with life, it rarely matters what our best intentions and plans are along the journey—life still remains an unpredictable mystery. To some, life is a dream—to others, a nightmare. As we travel through the journey of life, it's romantic to believe the path will always be smooth and wonderful. On average, life is a rhythmic balance or seesaw of ups and downs, peaks and valleys. However, an average life is not a reality for all of us. Some of us are severely tested by random acts of emotionally

INTRODUCTION

painful experiences. Much like an explosion going off in your soul, an inconceivable life event such as a tragedy or crisis will boggle the mind, leaving panic and despair in its path. Your world is forever altered by its effects.

It is not unusual for a crisis or tragedy to cause emotions or feelings to become so low that people fall victim to an entire life scarred by depression and grief. Unfortunately, some scars never heal, often becoming reasons for addictions, obsessions, and even crime. A crisis will threaten your sanity, making it very difficult to live a normal life. Depressed, you often find yourself consumed with dark, negative thoughts that develop like weeds growing out of control in your mind until they choke out all the hope within you. Life becomes so burdensome that you question yourself, wondering whether it is really worth living anymore. I was standing tip-toe on that very thin line, wavering to cross over to the other side of life. Emotionally drained and exhausted, you reach the tip of your breaking point. Dangling by a thread, most often you face a critical decision. Do I want to continue to hang on and try to survive this ordeal, or should I give up and surrender my mind and body to destruction? Sad to say, the breaking point is where I lived the better part of my life. I lived a nightmare of unforgiving emotional, and sometimes even physical, pain. It was a life I would have never chosen but one that chose me. Yet, I prevailed!

Instead of it destroying who I was, it defined who I am more than I could have ever imagined possible.

Though I was able to have a beautiful, healthy daughter, primarily this book reveals the extraordinary life I lived trying to manage the crises of my sons' disabilities—their struggle to survive a rare disease—along with my struggle to care for them.

Maybe, like I once was, you are having difficulty overcoming the death of a loved one, or maybe you're dealing with murder, victimization, betrayal, a fatally ill child, or any upheaval you feel you can't possibly handle alone anymore. Please, don't lose hope. Hope is life's mysterious human wonder that unites your fragile, mortal inabilities with the spiritual and all-powerful abilities of God. He will change you spiritually and He will give you a reason and purpose to live a peaceful and acceptable life.

I hope you are convinced that you are never hopeless. It is always your choice to believe in a better day.

Hold on to that grain of hope for just one more day, for just one more moment, for maybe just one more second.

Part 1

THE JOURNEY

I loved my husband-to-be at first sight. Well, at least what I believed to be love. He was just ten years old and I was nine. We were exactly one year apart, both born on March 2nd. In retrospect, I can safely say it was puppy love. The young man's name was Howard Jack, but the kids in the neighborhood nicknamed him Jackyboy. His father and namesake they called Jacky. I guess they didn't want to call my husband-to-be Jacky Junior, so they just added "boy" to his nickname.

The first time I saw Jackyboy, he was riding on the back of a pickup truck with my cousin, Roger. They worked as helpers for a local huckster selling watermelons, or as they liked to call them, "watermelos." Hucksters were street vendors who rode through neighborhoods in open-body trucks filled mostly with produce. Hucksters and helpers yelled out what type of produce they were selling to eagerly awaiting shoppers. Jackyboy and Roger were a good working team and had a strong friendship. Both boys would jump off the back of the truck after a good melon was selected by a customer, then carry the melon to the customer's house and collect the payment.

I was eager for Roger to come home from work that day because I wanted to talk to him about Jackyboy. Roger happened to be my favorite male cousin. People often told us that we looked alike. We were the same age and we got along very well. I loved spending my summers with my cousins—Roger and his younger sister, Darla. I was also fortunate to be their mother's namesake. She would tease me by saying I was her favorite niece. I loved my Aunt Delores and spending nights at her house during the summer months.

I pestered Roger to tell me more about the boy who was working with him on the watermelon truck. I used to follow him around hoping he would tell me something about Jackyboy. Roger just looked at me with disgust and in a gruff voice said, "Leave him alone, he doesn't like girls." It was obvious that Roger wasn't going to discuss Jackyboy with me. And Jackyboy was never going to find out through Roger that I liked him, because Roger wasn't going to tell him. And that was that.

One other time I saw Jackyboy sitting on the sidewalk in front of his house. Other than once on the truck, that was the only time I saw him as a young girl. I was forced to forget my crush. Out of sight, out of mind as they say. However, as fate would have it, four years later Jackyboy graduated from grade school and ended up in the same junior high school that I attended. By then, he had matured into a very handsome teenager, and the torch I carried for him rekindled as soon as I saw him. He was tall with wavy dark brown hair, flawless tan skin, and light brown dreamy eyes. He was always well-groomed and well-dressed. He had a cool walk and was quite a striking young man. As they would say today, he had "swag."

Thinking of him as a prospective boyfriend, I thought he would be the perfect catch. It was obvious that other girls shared the same sentiments. However, I didn't notice Jackyboy giving any particular girl special attention. In retrospect, I think he enjoyed being sought after.

Sometimes I would peer out of my classroom window during boys' gym period to watch him play basketball on the basketball court. Oh! I almost forgot to mention that he had very nice legs. I purposely tried to get him to notice me every chance that I could, showing up wherever I knew he would be. It took several months before I finally got his attention at the annual Fourth of July street dance. I wore a beautiful bright emerald green, Asian-style silk pantsuit. My outfit stood out in the crowd and looked very pretty. I still love silk clothing and wear it whenever I can; I guess some things never change.

I jokingly share with people that my husband never knew what hit him. He wasn't aware of me lovingly stalking him. The outfit must have worked. I am happy to say it didn't take long before we started dating; at the time he was fifteen years old and I fourteen.

Our dating pretty much consisted of us walking each other home after school, kissing when no one was looking, and sneaking away to neck at one of my married sisters' houses. I had two sisters who married very young. Living their own busy lives, they had children and their own apartments. I was happy to be their babysitter because it made it convenient for Jackyboy to sneak over to see me. My sisters didn't mind me sneaking him over, but my parents would have killed me if they'd found out (figuratively speaking). My dad might have literally fought with Jackyboy. The word on the street was that my father was crazy; hands off his five daughters or else risk peril. They were probably right.

After about two years of basically dating in secret and falling in love, we became intimate. It's funny how being immature can convince you that risks are all right to take. But immaturity is innocent and pure and we all go through

THE JOURNEY

it as kids. I was naïve and didn't know anything about birth control. Jackyboy was my first sexual relationship, my only real romantic relationship. My parents were old-fashioned and they never counseled me on the "birds and the bees," or much of anything else a young girl should know. I actually didn't know what was involved during a menstrual cycle and the fertilization process. Incredible as this might seem, I didn't know how girls became pregnant. I am embarrassed to admit how immature I was. I was just responding to my natural feelings and desires without understanding the responsibilities or repercussions of my actions. It is not my intention to make excuses. I fully understood that I wasn't supposed to be intimate because I wasn't married. It just didn't seem to matter at the time. It didn't take very long before I became pregnant. For some strange reason, we were both surprised when we found out. At the ages of eighteen and nineteen, I guess we never thought anything would happen to us. We were so, so wrong.

It's funny how being immature can convince you that risks are all right to take.

In my day, "decent girls" got married when they became pregnant. My mother strongly shared this belief and became very instrumental in enforcing my marriage to Jackyboy. As if it were yesterday, I remember her saying, "Well, you know what you have to do." Believe me, I knew just what she meant. Unfortunately, at eighteen I was still a child too. I had recently graduated high school, was attending a local business school, and worked as a tray girl at Montefiore Hospital. Jackyboy was working as a busboy at a drugstore in downtown Pittsburgh, and like me, he was attending a local college during the day. Our careers and, in some ways, our natural youthful development, were cut short. I was certainly not mature enough to be a wife, much less a mother, nor Jackyboy a husband and a father. We were two awkward kids under pressure doing what was expected of us.

As if it were yesterday, I remember her saying, "Well, you know what you have to do."

On October 16, 1965, just four months after graduating high school, we were whisked away by my parents. My heavy-on-the-gas-pedal mother sped us off to our wedding, and in a moment's notice, we were united in marriage at the house of a local minister who we had just met for the first time. It was a scary experience getting married, but my mother didn't offer me any other choices, and Jacky just went along with it. I was afraid to tell my father I was pregnant because he was very stern and I was intimidated by him. But looking back, there was no way that he didn't know. Why else would I be getting married? Though at that point, I felt safe because I was getting married, and he couldn't do or say anything to Jackyboy or me.

The entire ceremony was planned with just a straightforward, impromptu telephone call to the preacher and my favorite female cousin, Darla. My mother coordinated the time and place with my family and my soon-to-be husband's parents. Obviously, our wedding was quick and simple, without any frills. I looked quite stunning! I was built very thin (weighing only 87 pounds and not yet showing) and had a head full of long, dark brown hair that matched my dark brown eyes. As always, I enjoyed dressing in intense or bright colors. My wedding dress was a high-waist, hot pink, wool-blend dress with a beautiful wide satin waistband. Jackyboy, as handsome as always, wore a tailored navy suit.

We didn't have money for a formal wedding and we didn't send private invitations. Whoever wanted to come along for the wedding ceremony was certainly welcome. Darla, who was always there for me, became my maid of honor and her boyfriend, Bradley, was pleased to serve as best man. Probably because of such short notice, Jackyboy's father, his two brothers and three sisters, and my four sisters did not attend the wedding. His mother stood by smiling as my mother busily took charge. My mother was always bossy and was never open to anyone's opinion. Jackyboy and I stood there quietly as two obedient, innocent children fulfilling the wishes of my mother. This was our first time confronting adulthood. We had no idea what it meant to be pledged to each other and to be responsible for the outcomes of our own lives, yet we stood there willing to go for it. We got married.

We didn't have a reception, and the only gift we received was a red and white floral quilt handed to me—unwrapped—by my mother. After the wedding, we went to an ice cream store, Isaly's, sipped on strawberry milkshakes, and nibbled Lance's peanut butter cheese crackers. I still love the combination of a strawberry milkshake with peanut butter cheese crackers. It really was a happy day for us and we felt like grownups for the first time. We had no idea what it meant to be married, but we were eager to learn as we went along.

After the realization of leaving the protection of my parent's home settled in, I became filled with anxiety and fear wondering if Jackyboy would be able to take care of me like my dad had always done. My father worked several jobs to provide for our family, and by this time,

THE JOURNEY

Jackyboy only had an entry-level job at Westinghouse Electric Company. My mother, on the other hand, was a stay-at-home mom caring for my four sisters and me. Both of my parents were strict and kept us girls close to the nest or to their breast. Now without them, Jackyboy and I were either going to "sink or swim." I'll let you be the judge.

Jacky and I had so much in common, aside from one distinct difference—I was outgoing and he was introverted. I think that is why we were attracted to each other. Especially because it was on the same day, our birthdays were special to us. We always celebrated by getting dressed up and going out to dinner. One year, my sisters threw us a surprise party and every year we were so sure they were going to give us a surprise party again. However, they didn't. So, like we did often did, we spoiled each other instead.

We both had a natural appetite for top shelf. Whatever Jacky wanted, I didn't object to it unless it was too far out of our budget, and he felt the same way about me. You might say we were our own check and balance system.

Even though we were very young, my husband and I sincerely loved each other. We wanted to be responsible, caring parents and raise a medium-size family. We promised each other to stay committed to our marriage for our children's sake, even if we fell out of love with each other. That had always been the staying power of our relationship and marriage.

We rented a second floor spare bedroom in the home of Mrs. Redmond. She was a friend of Jackyboy's grandmother. Mrs. Redmond was a widow who lived alone for many years. She was probably in her seventies. She was a beautiful, freckled, and fair-skinned woman, with silver, wavy hair that softly framed her aging face. Mrs. Redmond had a short and stocky stature with a slight curve in her back. She would walk from room to room very slowly, but mostly sat in her favorite chair all day in front of the picture window in the living room. Her kindness made it a joy to live in her home. I loved talking with Mrs. Redmond while Jackyboy was at work; she was good company and I learned many things from her. She treated us as though we were her own; she never had any children, so it worked out well for all of us. She would sit in her favorite chair smiling at us, the two young newlyweds. To her, we were children playing house; to us, she was a nurturing mother who provided a safe and comfortable place to live. We loved Mrs. Redmond like a mother, and in return she allowed us to enjoy and live in her home, treating it as if it were our own. Her home was always well-maintained and clean; it was very pleasant

THE JOURNEY

living there like home sweet home. I will always cherish memories of Mrs. Redmond. She helped two tottering teenagers gain their legs.

She treated us as though we were her own; she never had any children, so it worked out well for all of us.

As my delivery date drew near, we knew we needed a larger place of our own before our baby was born. There wasn't enough space in our room to cram in three people; therefore, we decided to apply for a public housing apartment. Our application was approved, and when an apartment became available, we eagerly moved into it just in the nick of time. As it turned out, our apartment was conveniently situated across the courtyard from one of my older sisters, Raina, and her husband, along with their two children. Raina and I provided each other support. I babysat her kids and she babysat mine. Raina and I have always been the closest sisters, probably because we are close in age—only eighteen months apart. We've always lived near each other, and our children were playmates and close in age. Raina was a beautician by trade and the comedian of the family. She had many friends and most people enjoyed her quick wit and soft heart. She was very pretty too. Raina was extremely free-spirited and would give you the shirt off of her back; she literally did for most of her close friends. I was so thankful to be living near her; I knew she would help us in any way she could. With the unforeseen complications we were predestined to undergo, her presence in our lives was a preordained blessing straight from God. I can't thank her enough for her moral support and tender heart. Even now, she remains in my corner as both friend and sister, advocating on my behalf in whatever I venture out to do.

SONJA

March 17, 1966, just five months after I was married, my first child, a girl, entered the world healthy and beautiful. I had no idea childbirth labor pains would be so painful, yet the doctors said it was an easy delivery. It certainly didn't seem easy to me, although the warm cozy feeling I got when the nurse handed me my little baby girl, wrapped tightly head-to-toe like a gift, made it all worthwhile. It seemed unbelievable that I actually had a baby. I couldn't wait to peel back the blanket to see if she had all of her fingers and toes as I was always told you should do. Sure enough, they were all there as I had hoped, along with the cutest little mouth that made a tiny little circle whenever she yawned. Motherhood is an amazingly fulfilling experience. It seemed as though I had grown up, becoming a "woman" overnight. My emotions were very high, and I fell more deeply in love with my husband. I was on cloud nine with my small family; I had never felt such a dreamy experience like this before. It revealed a side of me I wasn't aware of.

GRAIN OF HOPE

We named our little bundle of joy Sonja Lynn—Sonja meaning "joy." Joy perfectly portrays what she brought to our lives the moment we saw her. We were very protective of our tiny baby. After bringing her home from the hospital, we didn't dare think of letting our precious little baby girl sleep in a separate bedroom. It seemed too far away. Therefore, I used an old remedy of my mother's by removing the largest drawer from our dresser, lining it with soft blankets for a mattress, and setting the drawer on top of the dresser where Sonja could sleep. This made it easy to watch her from our bed. This was Sonja's first crib, even though she had a perfectly fine crib in her room next to our bedroom. To my surprise, Sonja slept through the night, sucking on two fingers. Her fingers kept her quite content all night. Babies almost always wake during the night for feedings, so I was prepared and waiting with bottles and diapers on hand. However, I was the only one awake and waiting. I was quite worried that she slept through her nightly feeding. I called my parents first thing in the morning. My father answered the phone. I told him that Sonja didn't wake up for her nightly feeding. His response was that I was lucky to have a baby that allowed me to sleep during the night. His advice was not to wake her, but to let her sleep until she woke up on her own. I didn't expect that answer—it didn't seem like good

SONJA

advice—but I was accustomed to doing what he said to do so I followed it. It turned out to be good advice, because Sonja continued to be a healthy baby and grew normally without the nightly feeding.

After she outgrew the dresser drawer, we still didn't want her to sleep in her crib, alone in another room where we couldn't see her. Therefore, we let Sonja sleep with us in our bed. Lordy be, this was such a big mistake! Sonja squirmed around for what seemed like most of the night. Sometimes she would end up lying across the top of our heads. How did she get up there? We had many restless nights because every time we tried to put her in her crib, she cried and screamed. She hated her crib, and we couldn't bear to hear her cry, so we put her back in our bed.

During a visit to the well-baby clinic, I discussed our sleeping arrangement dilemma with the pediatrician. He explained that in order to stop the crying, we would have to let her cry until she settled down to sleeping in her crib. We took the doctor's advice and let her cry. Sonja would cry very loud, shake her crib and jump up and down. She was determined to sleep with us. At first we would give in and put her back in our bed. Then one day, I decided to go for it and let her cry. It seemed as though she cried for a couple of hours, stopping in-between to catch her breath and rest. Finally, she became exhausted and eventually drifted off to sleep. This bedtime behavior continued for several weeks; it was awful listening to her cry.

Bedtime at our house was quite an ordeal. No doubt this ten-month old baby was smart enough to know how to control her love-struck parents. I didn't have to get up for work, but I did want to spend some time with my husband in the evening since he worked during the day. Like most parents with young children, her bedtime was our time together. It is the only timeout for parents where they can enjoy peace and quiet and adult conversation. We really felt sorry for her, so it took willpower not to rescue our unhappy baby. But as it turned out, the doctor was right; one day it stopped and she willingly slept in her crib without a fight.

Sonja developed normally—playing, walking, and exploring her small world, our apartment. She was a funny and stubborn little girl. She was also mischievous. One day she piled a bunch of Vaseline in her hair. I had to use laundry detergent to get it out. During her stubborn phase, or what I call the "I'll fix you" phase, she would bang her head on something when she didn't get her way or do the opposite of what you wanted her to do. She quickly learned how to manipulate us. Other than maybe catching a cold or falling like normal children, she stayed healthy and learned to do things as other children her age. She truly was a joy, and Jackyboy and I looked forward to playing with her every day.

I always loved children and it was natural for me to want more. Jackyboy wanted more children, too. We were both very thrilled with our small family, but we wanted very much to have a larger one. Somehow, the fact that we were quite young didn't seem to matter.

GLENN

Once there was a six-year-old girl who got a pretty brown-faced, big-eyed baby doll for Christmas. She was so happy to have her new doll. She named her Doris because her name was Dolores. One day while playing, she accidentally cut her doll's tiny thumb off. She was so sad and unhappy with what she had done that she went to the window, held her doll up to the sky and prayed to God to put the thumb back on. Could God be so real to such a young child? And was it possible for her to know if God could hear her?

She promised God that if He put back the thumb she would keep it a secret.

Maybe life is predestined, because just fourteen years later the similarities were uncanny.

Two years after Sonja was born, I gave birth to a baby boy on August 14, 1968. It was just perfect: we had a boy and a girl. Unlike my excitement with my first child, my son's reception into the world was quite different from my daughter's. It was not the same warm feeling I had experienced before, because when I looked at him, I had this strange feeling that something was wrong. The bridge of his nose was extremely flat, and as I pulled back the blanket that was tightly wrapped around his tiny body, I noticed that the large toe on his right foot was bent downward as if it were broken. It upset me, but I held back my sad feelings to avoid spoiling the celebration of our baby boy with the rest of the family. However, Jackyboy expressed concern, too. He shared with me his prayer that our son would be mentally normal, despite his peculiar appearance.

We named him Glenn Thomas. Unlike Sonja who was born bald, Glenn had a head full of dark brown curls that matched his big dark brown eyes. Other than his flat nose and bent toe, he appeared to be a healthy baby.

Upon discharge from the hospital, I was instructed by the doctor to make an appointment with an orthopedic doctor at the Children's Hospital within six weeks to correct Glenn's toe. The doctor didn't seem concerned about his nose, or at least he didn't mention anything to me. I thought Glenn's nose and toe were a temporary condition that would be corrected somehow. It grieved me to see that he had a problem. I prayed during the night that everything would work out fine.

GLENN

When we brought Glenn home to meet his big sister, she was very happy to see him. Sonja never competed with her brother for attention because of the new baby on the block. She was eager to run back and forth through our apartment to help me with his feedings and changing his diapers.

Glenn and Sonja shared the same room. By now, she had a regular bed and Glenn went straight to the bassinet until it was time to put him in the crib. We learned our lesson from our previous experience with Sonja and made sure not to let Glenn sleep with us.

Following the doctor's instructions, I made an appointment with the orthopedic doctor at the clinic. On the day of the appointment, I went to the hospital alone, leaving Sonja in the care of Raina. Jacky had to go to work (it was time to drop the "boy" from his name because he was a man now).

The clinic was on the first floor of the Children's Hospital. I walked into a large sterile open area sectioned off by curtains into small exam cubicles. It was full of crying babies and children and busy moms caring for and keeping their restless children calm. The nurses and doctors busied about and talked among themselves as though the parents were invisible. Everything was routine with them: not much caring, just duty.

After waiting about two hours, I was called to an examination area with Glenn. The doctor, who solemnly introduced himself as Dr. Lane, asked me several personal, family-related questions, and then proceeded to carefully examine Glenn. After the doctor's initial examination, he wrote an order to have x-rays taken of Glenn's feet. I was instructed to go down the hall to the radiology department waiting room, which I did, and again waited patiently with Glenn for another hour.

When our turn came, I handed Glenn to a nurse who took him into the x-ray room. After the x-ray, we were instructed to go back to the examining room and wait for the doctor. Upon viewing Glenn's x-rays and discussing them amongst several other doctors, Dr. Lane turned to me. He began explaining that Glenn not only had a "hammer toe," but that the anklebones in both feet were also out of alignment. He continued to say that in order to correct the deformity he was going to put each foot in a cast, from feet to knees. The procedure involved stretching the anklebones downward, then stretching them back up again to their normal position in hopes of properly aligning the bones. While the doctors continued to talk medical terms with each other, I sat there dumbfounded, my mind in a fog. Dr. Lane continued to say that Glenn had a very rare bone disease named Conradi's Disease.

The word "disease" sounded scary. My heart sunk. I had spent the better part of my day waiting around in this strange, unfriendly place, carrying a baby bag, purse, and baby only to be disappointed with hearing unexpected bad news that my baby had a disease. During the sixties, doctors didn't give you detailed explanations; there were no fancy educational brochures or video presentations. You just accepted what doctors told you, pretended to understand, and refrained from asking many questions. Actually, I didn't even know what to ask.

Of course, Google wasn't around back then. I couldn't pick up my iPhone and look up the disease like I can now. It wasn't until decades later I learned from Google searches that the proper name for Conradi's Disease is Conradi-Hunermann syndrome named after two German doctors, Erich Conradi and Carl Hunermann. Boy babies rarely survive the disease.

Conradi's Disease is so rare that when Glenn was diagnosed, there was not a lot of information about the disease. The disease was a total mystery to me, of course, and even to most of the doctors who examined Glenn. The primary characteristic of the disease is the deterioration of cartilage and connective tissues in the body, preventing normal bone growth. I was too young and inexperienced in medical matters to understand the seriousness of the disease and the long-term effects it would have on Glenn. There was nothing I could say or do but let them put casts on my little baby's feet.

Sitting there waiting for the doctor to perform the casting, I felt utterly helpless and puzzled. The nurse entered the room to assist the doctor with the procedure. She brought with her all of the supplies needed for wrapping a cast. Dr. Lane entered the room, sat on a stool in front of me, and put on the casts while I held Glenn on my lap.

First, he painted both legs from knees to feet with a red solution called Benzene. It pained me to watch as the doctor forced each foot in a downward position. Then, he slowly wrapped them with a roll of cotton wrap. Next, a white netted material was dipped in water and then meticulously wrapped just below the knee. I didn't expect them to be so far up his legs. Just watching this made me light-headed and I felt ill. I never experienced anything like this. Imagine both of your little baby's legs dangling from the weight of ugly heavy casts. He looked so pitiful; I had to gulp back tears because I didn't want anyone to know that I was very upset.

GLENN

It seemed no big deal to the doctor because after he was finished casting Glenn, he told me to make an appointment with the nurse for changing his casts. And then he quickly moved on to the next patient much like an assembly line. The whole ordeal was weakening and too difficult for me to even think about. How could I take my baby home to our family looking like this? They were supportive, of course, but how was I supposed to talk about something I didn't even understand? I felt so sorry for my little fellow. Glenn was soon to be two months old, and I was at least glad he was unaware of what had just happened to him. I eagerly gathered our things and quickly walked out of the hospital. I could not wait any longer. Finally, the tears started to flow. I cried all the way to the bus stop. I guess it was now safe enough to express my feelings.

The casts made it more difficult to carry Glenn and the diaper bag to the bus stop; they were heavy and awkward and kept getting in my way. We had been at the hospital for over four hours. I was sapped of most of my strength and hungry because I hadn't eaten anything all day. I had no idea I would be gone this long. I still needed to pick up Sonja from the babysitter, go home and prepare dinner for my family, and be ready to face Jacky with the news.

When Jacky got home that evening from work, I showed him what the doctors had done to our little son's legs and feet, while explaining as best I could what the doctors explained to me. Jacky was shocked and upset by what he saw and heard and by what I had suffered through that day. When I told him Glenn had Conradi's Disease, his reaction to the word "disease" was much like mine: baffled. He wanted to know everything about the disease, but I didn't have many answers because the doctors didn't offer any. I didn't know what to say to him. I could see the fear and frustration on Jacky's face. It was as though I was looking into a mirror. And like a broken mirror, our joy was shattered into tiny pieces.

Having to accept something you have no power to change is the worst feeling, especially when it concerns your child, because your children depend on you for everything. I don't mean to minimize a father's love, but I believe the love a mother has for a child surpasses everything. Like most mothers, it really hurt my heart, my soul, and my spirit to see this happen to my child. Glenn was in trouble, and neither Jacky nor I could help him. I hid my emotions as best I could from Jacky and the people around me. I pretended to have it all together and didn't want others to know that internally I was in turmoil. I knew Jacky had to work and I didn't want him to sit at work all day worrying about his family, so I always tried to make things appear as though everything would be okay. I feared my family would fall apart if I didn't keep my emotions under control. I saved my tears for private times during the day and under the cover of darkness at night where no one could see. I was young and frightened and desperately trying to balance Glenn's health issues and the daily demanding needs of a husband and young family.

I was brought up as a Christian, the fourth of five sisters. I have vivid memories of my mother sending us to church, whether we wanted to go or not. In retrospect, I am glad that she did. For reasons unbeknownst to me, when I was a little girl, I somehow really believed there was a God or some power beyond mankind. I didn't know what it meant to serve Him; I just did what was expected of me in church. I bowed my head, closed my eyes when I was told to pray, and sang when it was time to sing. In Sunday school, I was taught that God lived in Heaven far above the clouds. He was good, He could perform miracles, and He loved me. I didn't quite know what a miracle was, but I knew God could do something no one else could do. That is why as a little girl I prayed for my baby doll's thumb.

Much like with most religions, you practiced what you were brought up to practice by your parents. I didn't doubt or question Christianity. I hoped God could help my son; I believed He could. I was glad I was taught that there was somewhere to turn for help. I somehow knew that without believing in God, everything would be hopeless. I was yearning for help, yearning for answers from God. So, during the night, I would talk to God under my breath because I didn't want Jacky to hear me talking to something he couldn't see. If God could hear me and my heart—I thought if I persistently begged—He would heal Glenn's problems and shortly everything would be okay. I just hoped or imagined that Christianity was right, because I was desperate. And when you are desperate, it can't hurt anything to hope in God. Being raised a Christian, I believe it took hope to open my heart and mind to believe for myself in the unseen God of the Bible. When you pray to God as much as I did, maybe He is bound to manifest. Hope was the bridge that connected me to a faith in God.

I somehow knew that without believing in God, everything would be hopeless.

Just three months after Glenn was born, I became pregnant for a third time. I was taking birth control, but clearly it had failed. The timing wasn't good either, because as you can see my hands were full already with a toddler, a sick baby, a husband, and household chores.

Pregnant, I continued catching buses back and forth to the clinic to take Glenn to get his casts changed. A typical

GLENN

morning for me was getting dressed, dressing Sonja and Glenn, fixing us breakfast, preparing a diaper bag and a bag of some things for Sonja, and dropping Sonja off at my sister's house across the court or catching a bus to my mother-in-law's house. Sometimes, I had to take them both to the clinic. It was almost impossible to handle both little ones on the bus, but I had no other choice. I clumsily carried Glenn in my arms, and being a toddler, Sonja walked slowly by my side. I guess you can say I was learning how to be patient. Unfortunately, most times Sonja was often left at a sitter for the sake of convenience.

Visits to the hospital meant waiting hours to see the doctor, waiting for x-ray results, and watching the doctor go through the tedious process of changing casts. Since babies grow fast, Glenn's casts were changed every month. It was routine to sit in the waiting area hungry and tired for about three hours. On days that I brought both Sonja and Glenn, they would often become cranky and sleepy as we waited to be called. It was a little too much to ask of small children. This is when I had to use my newfound patience.

During each monthly appointment, the doctor continued flexing his feet more downward as they changed the casts. As Glenn grew larger, so did his casts. He became heavier as did the baby inside of me. Somehow, I struggled through the day and made it back home afterwards. I still had to prepare dinner, clean up afterwards, and care for my family even though I was physically and mentally beside myself. Every month, I had to look forward to repeating the same trip to the Children's Hospital without an end in sight or good news. I tried not to complain. I pretended as though it did not bother me because I believed it would soon come to an end. Nothing was going to be more pressing or important than Glenn being okay. The thought of him eventually being okay motivated me to do whatever it took. Hope was alive within me.

The stress of being almost eight months pregnant and trying to lug diaper bags, a baby, and a toddler back and forth to the clinic on the bus became almost unbearable. I was relieved when I could leave Sonja with my sister or mother-in-law. Glenn's casts were becoming heavier and more uncomfortable for him. I'm sure forcing his foot downward was a strain too. Just imagine having your toes and feet pointed downward in a ballerina position all day. That couldn't be easy; it's unnatural and strains the foot.

Aside from all the other concerns, Glenn, soon to be a one-year-old, was still not sitting up alone or crawling like most babies his age. He didn't have much control of his body like he should have. I assumed it was because the weight of the casts made it hard to balance himself. As the

GLENN

months went by, he became extremely fussy and wanted me to hold him most of the time. His constant crying was very irritating. We were both irritated. To stop the crying, I carried him around all day. Believe me, it wasn't easy having a big tummy while carrying around an almost one-year-old baby in awkward and heavy casts. Yet, I managed to carry him even while performing housework, cooking dinner, and caring for Sonja, an active toddler. You can see why I looked forward to the bedtime break when Jacky and I could be alone together.

After everyone was asleep, I stayed awake in the dark praying and crying until I finally drifted off to some much-needed sleep. Another concern of mine that had nothing to do with Glenn's cast was why he couldn't hold his head up straight. It wobbled from side to side. When I tried to prop him up to sit, his head would topple over and his body would follow. I didn't understand why his legs would have any effect on his head. Whenever I tried to steady his head, he cried and showed a pained expression. Something was terribly wrong! When I brought this up to the pediatrician, he sort of shrugged it off and didn't seem to be concerned. He tried to reassure me by saying that some babies develop slower than others and we didn't need to worry. He didn't address my concerns about Glenn being in pain either. I guess the doctors just thought Glenn was a big crybaby or that I was an over-concerned mother. When I reflect back on that day, I don't think the doctors really bothered to find out the problem. What were their reasons not to? Maybe they thought his feet were more of a priority or they had too much pride to admit they didn't really know what to do.

As the days went by, it seemed as though the only thing that comforted Glenn was resting his little head on my shoulder. I was still carrying him around all day and I had enough practice. I was quite skilled at it. I could do almost all my chores with Glenn on my hip or shoulder, even at nine months pregnant. The only thing I couldn't master was holding Glenn while I ironed clothes. He held on for dear life too, in the way that baby animals grasp onto their mother as she carries them from place to place. Each time I tried to lay him in his crib, he would start crying. On occasion when I was able to lay him down, I made sure that he could see me. He watched my every move. I felt sorry for my helpless little fellow. I started observing when and what was going on whenever Glenn cried. It was not just for normal feedings or diaper changes, but certain positions that his body was in made him more irritable. I had a gut feeling something was wrong; he wasn't crying just to be crying. Whatever the problem,

GLENN

it was not obvious to the doctors or me, but I was sure something else was wrong.

At a routine visit to the hospital, the doctor decided to take more x-rays of Glenn. Hopefully they had finally started listening to my complaints about his wobbly head and uncontrollable body. Surely you would think that an almost year-old child could sit alone by now.

During the x-ray, Glenn's head wobbled to the side and the x-ray captured a good view of his cervical spine, or neck area. The x-rays revealed the connecting bones of his cervical spine (cervical 2 and 3) were missing. This was an extremely fatal condition. Glenn had a broken neck—the reason for all that crying.

To explain how fatal his condition, consider that during a hanging, the neck bones or cervical bones are severed by a rope. In a normal neck, the cervical bones protect the cervical spinal cord. The cervical spinal cord helps control breathing. In Glenn's case, the bones required to protect the cervical spine as well as support the head were missing. This is why his head wobbled back and forth. It was also stretching his spinal cord out of its normal position every time he moved his head. It was a miracle that Glenn lived so long. Under normal circumstances he should have asphyxiated, or become paralyzed from the neck down. I didn't know any symptoms associated with a spinal cord injury, but you would think the doctors should certainly have known. Glenn was living all this time with a broken neck. There was no explanation as to why Glenn was still alive. Wouldn't you say if there are no scientific or medical reasons to be alive, there must be a reason unbeknownst to man? I believe this was my first encounter with the supernatural, a real miracle. Were the prayers I had been praying in the stillness of the night reaching God?

> *There was no explanation as to why Glenn was still alive.*

Upon discovering the seriousness of Glenn's condition, the hospital staff sprang into action. Glenn was immediately admitted to the hospital. Working quickly, the nurses secured a soft neck brace around his neck, laid him on a gurney and off they went. It was as if I was standing in the middle of fast-moving traffic as they whizzed by me. What in the world was happening? What were they going to do with my son? They didn't for one moment consider my feelings or acknowledge that I was a concerned mother who needed to know what was going on. They didn't seem to realize that I was just as upset and afraid as they would be if it were their child. It was as though the world was going on without me, and I was left standing in the hallway watching from the outside looking in.

After Glenn was settled into a room, I stayed with him until visiting hours were over and it was time to leave. I gathered all of our things, bent over to kiss his soft little cheeks, then slowly and reluctantly left him in the room. Walking down the long hallway was the loneliest moment ever. Leaving the hospital without my baby was very unsettling. I had been there all day without eating or checking on Sonja, completely unable to think about anything or anybody else but Glenn. My whole world was the very spot where I stood and I felt numb to everything around me. Only God knows how I eventually regained control of my thoughts, caught the bus, and headed toward home.

On the way home, as always, I composed myself before facing my family to deliver more bad news. I loved my family, and I couldn't bear to see them sad or upset. I always tried to spare them the pain I was suffering. So, I gave them a smaller dosage of what my day was like. I thought staying calm and picking and choosing what I wanted them to know was my way of protecting my family. I never wanted them to be unhappy or worried and they always naïvely followed my lead. Jacky was comfortable trusting my judgment, and as long as I was okay, he thought everything was okay. Because of Jacky's laid-back personality, he didn't appear to be too alarmed. He was not easy to gauge. He was glad to hear that the doctors had finally discovered the root of Glenn's problem. He was not present during the whole hospital scene; therefore, he was not aware of how crucial the situation had become. And besides, he didn't need to be preoccupied with worrying about his family while he was at work. I thought I could worry enough for the both of us.

I worried about Glenn all that night—thinking about how his little life had been in and out of the hospital, and now he had to stay there in a strange room overnight. The little guy had enough complications to deal with; now he had a life-threatening one. Problems were piling as high as they could for Glenn. He truly was a mystery for doctors to solve, and his prognosis didn't look good. The realization that he almost died was a shock. Of course, Glenn didn't understand the danger he was in; he was just an innocent little boy desiring to be with his family. I hoped the doctors found the problem soon, before it was too late.

The house felt empty without Glenn's presence. However, it was good to be back home and away from the hospital for a change. I prepared Sonja for bed and thanked God that she was too young to understand what was going on. It was a joy for us to see we had a normal bouncy and bubbly active little two-year-old. We had no reason to believe we wouldn't have a normal bouncy and bubbly active little boy one day, too. Jacky and I got ready for bed, and eventually we all settled down for the night. We talked about Glenn as we lie in bed in the darkness of our bedroom where it was safe to shed a tear and not see the fear in each other's faces. The darkness was always a good cover to hide the pain in our faces. We didn't often show each other how we felt. It seemed that we always wanted to appear courageous for each other, and at the first show of weakness, we would probably both fall apart. We were so young, so afraid, and so unaware of what was ahead of us.

The darkness was always a good cover to hide the pain in our faces.

But, we kept our feelings private and tried to be strong. It saddened us to know that Glenn was not sleeping in the next room in his own bed. Did the nurses have enough blankets covering him to keep him warm? Could the nurses hear him if he cried? It was painful not being able to look in on our baby and extremely difficult accepting that it was better for him to be in the hospital bed than in the comforts of his own bed.

Suddenly, during the wee hours of the next morning, the ring of our telephone awakened and startled us. A call during the night or early morning is always scary. We knew it was the hospital; who else would be calling us so early? Did something happen to Glenn during the night? Of course this was our first thought. I answered the telephone and it was a nurse. She called to get our verbal consent to put Glenn in traction. She emphasized the urgency of having it done immediately and that it could not wait any longer. What we knew about traction was putting your chin in a sling-like strap device to hold the head backwards. We understood the importance of immobilizing his neck. It seemed harmless and necessary; we knew that Glenn was in good hands. We consented to the procedure, said our goodbyes, hung up the phone, and went back to bed.

The next morning, I bathed Sonja, fed her breakfast, and put on her clothes. Then, Jacky and I dressed, ate, and got ready for the trip to the hospital. We took Sonja over to my sister's house. The convenience of her living across the court couldn't be more perfect. I really believe it was another preordained blessing. After we dropped Sonja off, we started for the bus. This was becoming a regular routine, leaving our little girl with someone else so that we could tend to her brother. We always felt guilty leaving Sonja, but we didn't have other options. A hospital was no place for a toddler, and besides, she was happier playing with her cousins and other children in the courtyard.

Figuratively speaking, during Sonja's formative years, she was a little, thirsty, sad-faced child, longing to get a drink of water from her parents. But instead, she stood there confused, watching them give water to her brothers and not to her. She had to use her own child-like imagination to determine why she was not given water, too. She lived many years with a dry sensation in her mouth and a deep thirst in her heart. Now if I may just substitute attention for water, I'm certain I've painted a regretfully accurate picture of Sonja's early impression of life.

Without realizing it, Jacky and I created an empty space between Sonja and us. Unforeseen, a crisis got in our way. During her most tender years, she only had portions of her parents when she needed, wanted, and deserved all of her parents. We always knew that our absorption with Glenn forced us to sacrifice time with Sonja. We cried about it all the time. However, our tears had no way of quenching her thirst.

How many times did Sonja fall down and we were not there to dry her tears and give her a comforting hug? How many times did she want to share something important to her with mommy and daddy? How many of her childhood questions never received answers? Did we miss the first time she was amazed by a colorful butterfly, flitting softly past her nose? Or, the day she was frightened by the bark of a dog when she reached out to give him a pet? Our precious memories and moments are hidden somewhere permanently in the past. And for everyone, the past, present, and future only exist one time. Our small family was going in all different directions, rarely feeling like the family togetherness we had hoped for.

Our precious memories and moments are hidden somewhere permanently in the past.

We were very anxious to get to the hospital to see Glenn. I wanted to be the first person he saw when he opened his eyes. I knew he would be happy to see us. We rushed off the bus and into the hospital. I walked very fast down the long hallways and didn't stop until I reached Glenn's room. Jacky was steps behind me. We didn't stop at the nurse's station, bathroom, or anywhere else. We wanted to make sure our son was all right.

GLENN

When I entered his room, I couldn't believe what was in front of me. What an awful scene! No one should ever witness without warning the sight of their child lying there with both arms and legs outstretched and tied down to bed rails. The top of his head was shaven bald. Next to his head was a plastic baggie that contained his beautiful curly locks of hair the nurses had shaved off. However, the most horrible and ghoulish thing of all was the two metal prongs that were hooked deep into his head, clamping onto his skull. These awful looking Frankenstein prongs were attached to a pulley-like device that lifted the weight of Glenn's skull off his neck. His bed was slanted upward at a 45-degree angle. He looked crucified. The fear and pitiful look on his innocent face still haunts me. It was more than any mother could bear. My first reaction was to throw myself out of the window behind his bed. I was outraged, out of control, and most likely out of my mind. I don't know what stopped me. Life lost all meaning in a moment. I started crying uncontrollably. Jacky just stood there in shock. The nurses heard me crying and rushed into the room to console me. The mere thought that our son hung there for hours alone and afraid was just awful. We had given our permission to do this horrible thing to our own child. I was extremely angry with the doctors and nurses. I felt as though they tricked us by taking advantage of our ignorance of this type of outrageous traction. They should have explained the procedure more thoroughly. We demanded to talk to the doctor who ordered this traction and we wanted to talk to him right away.

As I stood watching Glenn hang there, I'm sure I frightened him even more by the shocked expression on my face and my hysterical reaction. Sometime during this madness, I realized that I didn't want to upset Glenn. I knew I had to compose myself and get my emotions contained. I didn't want to make matters worse than what they were for him already. Thank God, thinking about my family has always prodded me to keep my emotions in check. All eyes were on me. I needed to help Glenn get through this, and I knew what I had to do. Jacky was always better at keeping his composure. He always internalized his pain as most men are socialized to do.

I didn't want to make matters worse than what they were for him already. Thank God, thinking about my family has always prodded me to keep my emotions in check.

The doctors came right away. The two neurologists who performed the procedure assured us that the decision to use this type of traction was crucial in saving Glenn's life

GLENN

and preventing paralysis. Life and paralysis! These words punched us in the stomach very hard. To the doctors this was just an everyday job; they appeared so matter-of-fact. They insisted Glenn stay in this monster-like traction until they could decide what to do next. What were they possibly going to do next?

After the doctors left, the nurses tried to reassure us that this type of traction was done all the time, but it was impossible to make me feel any better. That day is forever burned in my memory. It marked the beginning of an on-the-edge life for me, full of restless days, sleepless nights, anguish, and anxiety. Glenn's health problems were turning me inside out. I was screaming inside where no one could hear me. I was suffering in silence. I think of it as sliding uncontrollably into a weird, bewildered state of mind. There were days that I robotically went through the motions, but my heart wasn't there. Often, I was emotionless, with no answers, and the idea that I had no good reason to wake up every morning. I was an expert at hiding somewhere inside myself. I found this invisible hiding place whenever I needed to maintain a sense of normalcy on the outside for others to see. I had been telling myself that I didn't want to upset my family, and I constantly worried that if I let my façade slip for even just a little bit, they would fall apart too. Instead, I was the one falling apart.

I certainly had plenty of practice thinking I needed to wear two faces. The rationale I lived by was that my family needed me, and I loved them, and trying to keep them happy was one of my faces. Total emotional meltdown was the other face. Balancing two faces was a perpetual internal struggle. I am not saying that not revealing my innermost self was doing what was right; I just perceived it was right. In reality it was deception—a slow and methodical way of torturing myself.

The rationale I lived by was that my family needed me, and I loved them, and trying to keep them happy was one of my faces. Total emotional meltdown was the other face.

TYRONE

On August 26, 1969, Tyrone Douglas was born. From the moment I saw him, I knew without a doubt that he was in trouble too. It was obvious from just looking at his peculiar little face that the disease had struck again. Tyrone's condition appeared to be even more severe than his brother's. His eyes were crossed and rolled around in their sockets, unable to focus on anything. His tongue dangled slightly from his mouth. His nose was very flat and odd shaped, even flatter than Glenn's nose. When the nurses placed him in my arms, I could feel his body was spastic and rigid, nothing like the soft and cuddly feeling of my other babies. As I examined the little guy's body, I found I had to pry his fingers up to open his hands. They would close again if I didn't hold them open. He kept his arms very tight to his body and bent at the elbow. If you pulled his arms down by his side, they were so spastic that they would pop back up again. All of his toes and fingers were normal, but he certainly wasn't.

His symptoms were quite different from Glenn's. Glenn was never spastic and always maintained control of his eyes and tongue. However, both babies cried a lot; they had this in common. A pacifier did the trick for Tyrone. And it had to be in his mouth at all times. Glenn did not cry at the very beginning, so he never needed a pacifier. Besides, I had carried him around on my hip all day before Tyrone was born. But now, I had a three-year-old, a one-year-old, and a newborn baby. No way could I carry anyone on my hip or anywhere else all day.

I dreamed this baby would ease some of the sadness in our family left by Glenn's situation. We needed to be happy about something. I had no reason to believe that this baby wouldn't be normal. You can't imagine how broken-hearted I was when my dream bubble suddenly popped. How could a rare disease strike twice? No one thought this would be possible. It was inconceivable to think that I had two babies born with severe birth defects that are supposedly rare.

A new baby is supposed to fill your home with joy and excitement. We all could have used a large dose of good feelings. Don't misunderstand me; we were very happy that Tyrone arrived safely. He was very much wanted. I just knew that this little guy and the rest of us were going to have to battle some storms very similar to his older brother.

TYRONE

I believe most parents of children with special needs have an innate ability to deal with their children's problems while experiencing unconditional love for their child. Their condition can be very overwhelming and heart wrenching, but we endure because they need us and we love them so much.

Most everything has an end; even emotions have endings. When something is funny, eventually you stop laughing; you even stop being angry. But the consuming sorrow I felt in my soul had no end. It was with me every moment of the day. The effects of my sons' disease were virtually impossible to deal with.

Sometimes the tension was so intense that it seemed to be squeezing my brain; my head felt tight all day. Often, during the night while I was trying to sleep, my tongue would swell and I couldn't keep it in my mouth. I used to gag, actually feeling like I was going to choke on my own saliva at times. I never told anyone about what was happening to me. I can't even say if I was really ill or if it was my mind playing tricks on me. It is amazing what fear and continuous worry and stress will do to you physically and mentally.

I still managed my life and gave my children and husband very good care. I never became unraveled or detached to the point that I couldn't cope with the day-to-day matters of life. Remember, my meltdown was not visible to the naked eye. It was hidden deep, deep down inside of me as if it was a valuable treasure that I made sure no one could find. I was able to function in my dysfunctional world.

One part of my life depicted sanity and the other was insanely impossible. It had become normal to live with a desperate heart, always teetering on the brink of collapse. In retrospect, I should have sought out counseling, but I wasn't mature enough or knowledgeable enough to seek professional care. What you don't know can truly hurt you. I reached deep into my soul for strength and hope. I believed that there was a God who cared and I looked forward to His help. I don't believe God brings the storm, but He certainly gives the energy needed to weather any storm.

One part of my life depicted sanity and the other was insanely impossible. It had become normal to live with a desperate heart, always teetering on the brink of collapse.

Needless to say, it was confirmed by x-ray that Tyrone had Conradi's Disease too. Next, we wondered if he had a broken neck too. He would need further examination and

TYRONE

x-rays before we would know. Just to play it safe, doctors placed Tyrone in a soft neck brace after his six-week well baby checkup. Unlike Glenn, Tyrone became more and more spastic as time went on. It was even difficult to give him a bath. In contrast, Glenn was too floppy and Tyrone was too rigid. Tyrone could not move and had to be repositioned often because he perspired profusely when he lay in one spot too long. It was a challenge to feed him because he couldn't control his tongue very well or suck milk through a regular baby bottle nipple. A nurse suggested I try premature baby nipples for his bottles. These nipples worked out better because they were made of a softer rubber and didn't require much effort to suck out the formula.

The doctors were right in suspecting that Tyrone had missing vertebrae as well. Sure enough, Tyrone's situation was critical. Because of the urgency of their conditions, the doctor immediately scheduled surgeries. Each of my sons was going to have the cervical bones in their necks fused together to rebuild their necks and hopefully prevent death. Tyrone was more fortunate because he was diagnosed early. Glenn had been living with this condition much longer, so he was scheduled to have his surgery first. Tyrone would undergo surgery shortly thereafter.

LIFE-THREATENING SURGERIES

I was on pins and needles the night before Glenn's surgery. This was quite an ordeal for a young family to go through. I cried on God's shoulders for what seemed like the entire night until I was exhausted enough to fall to sleep. My only comfort and peace of mind came from talking to God. I hoped and prayed that I would get through this traumatic situation in one piece. I really couldn't wrap my mind around the fact that my sons could possibly die. They were just babies! My baby dying! I had never imagined experiencing anything this frightening. The thought of my little boys put into some sort of deep sleep, being hooked up to all kinds of equipment, and having their flesh cut open seemed horrific. We were made aware that it was a life-threatening, delicate, and uncertain surgery. I know I was totally unprepared if the surgery didn't work out or worse, proved fatal. I hoped God's presence would be there this time as He had been so many times before. My hope was leaning on His imaginary arms for comfort and reassurance.

GRAIN OF HOPE

The next morning, I woke up feeling the same numbness and intoxication that I had felt many times before. Even more so because every problem, every nail-biting event added more emotional weight onto what was already too heavy a load. Of course, I was on edge—anyone would be. It had become difficult to determine whether this was a nightmare or the real thing. After a while it really didn't matter.

As I went through the motion of getting ready for the crisis of the day, my body kept doing what was right, but my mind was all over the place. In my usual boggled state of mind, I dressed Sonja, gave her breakfast, and packed her bag for the babysitter again. Jacky was still in the bedroom quietly getting dressed. He looked as troubled as I felt. We had never been around anyone so seriously ill, much less waiting through an operation. And to make matters worse, it was going to be our precious children. We had no idea what to expect. We just went about doing what we had to do, completely afraid and unsure. Everything had become too overwhelming. It was truly a miracle to put one foot in front of the other that day.

As you could imagine, the ride to the hospital was solemn; you could hear a pin drop. Jacky was naturally a very introverted person, only talking when he had something to say. Unlike me, the opposite: extraverted and

LIFE-THREATENING SURGERIES

talkative. However, both Jacky and I were speechless this time; we suffered in silence and didn't dare break down and pour our feelings out to each other. By now, we were both experts at keeping our feelings inside, unable to share with each other how we really felt. I realize now that this is unhealthy and abnormal in a relationship. We sort of dragged through each day, saying necessary words and being intimate mostly out of routine. Our relationship had sadly evolved into one of obligation. We did not have much time for ourselves, passion, or romance. It was a marriage overwhelmed with barriers and distractions that interfered with our ability to express and develop intimately as a couple. Our lives were put on hold; we only knew how to live in a crisis situation, with our everyday lives revolving around the problems of our children. Jacky was busy working and doing what he could do to support his family, assisting with the care of our children when he was off work. I was busy with everything else.

Our silence was our agreement that everything was okay. Jacky was showing me he was still holding things down in order to keep me from breaking down, and I know I was certainly trying to do the same. Unexpectedly, we were gradually becoming two broken-down pressure cookers getting ready to blow at any time.

GRAIN OF HOPE

We arrived at the hospital early. We wanted to make sure we could spend some quality time with Glenn before they came to take him into surgery. He innocently lay there while we hugged and kissed all over him. He was too young to know what was going to happen to him. He wasn't afraid. He willingly went with them when they came for him. It was as though I was giving him away, maybe never to return. Was the surgery going to cure all of Glenn's problems? Or was this going to be the last time I would see him alive? We knew the risks, and they were not favorable. He could become paralyzed for life from the neck down or die if the surgery wasn't successful. Out of the two, which option would we be prepared to live with? The answer was neither one.

I knew Jacky, like me, was extremely worried and filled with doubt. It was impossible not to be. The anxiety and anticipation waiting on the results of the surgery were unimaginable. You sit and wait, wait and sit. You put your head in both hands, you walk the floors, you close your eyes and you think, and think, and think. As the hours go slowly by, you try to picture what is going on in the operating room. It was just agonizing! But inside me was a low burning glimmer of hope that God would perform another miracle.

LIFE-THREATENING SURGERIES

The news came at last; the doctors told us the surgery went very well. Thank you, Lord! Symphony music couldn't have sounded as soothing as those precious few words. Oh, what a relief! I could literally feel all the tension that had hardened inside my body melt like ice. At last, we could leave that imprisoned waiting room to relax and get something to eat. Glenn was safely recovering in the hospital intensive care unit. Our little boy was going to be okay. God allowed everything to turn out right, and He gave us the strength we needed to endure what seemed to be an impossible situation. Glenn surviving the surgery gave us the hope we needed for Tyrone. However, our optimism was overshadowed by the reality that we were going to suffer through the same tormenting experience again.

Since Tyrone was placed in a soft neck brace early, we were spared another monstrous traction scene. Our sons were in the Children's Hospital at the same time. Tyrone was at one end of the hall and Glenn at the other. It was just another one of life's inconveniences, going up and down the halls from room to room visiting, feeding and playing with each son.

One week after Glenn's surgery, our lives became a rerun of an old movie, waiting, while Tyrone was in surgery. And as with Glenn, we were told Tyrone's surgery went well.

The pressure was off; we survived two very tense, nail-biting events. Thank God, no more surgeries. Our sons' problems were finally coming to an end, and we could soon go on as a normal family with a normal life.

Glenn and Tyrone stayed in the hospital for a short while to recuperate. Because they were young, the doctors assured us that they would heal quickly. I must admit, when they were both in the hospital it gave me a well-deserved break to decompress. I didn't have to coordinate so many baths or juggle feedings. I had more time to spend with Jacky and Sonja and personal time to do some things that I otherwise couldn't, such as come and go at will to visit friends and family.

Let's see, where are we? I'm twenty-two years old, married with three very young children, two of whom have special needs. It was obvious that I had quite a challenge ahead of me. How do you even make plans when you have no idea when or if your children are going to get better? When would going back and forth to doctor's appointments cease? It never occurred to me that things could get worse. Nothing prevented me from believing that Glenn and Tyrone would one day walk and talk and be like other children. I hoped they would. The doctors never told me they wouldn't. I hoped eventually everything would

LIFE-THREATENING SURGERIES

just be fine and all of this would be in the past. I was so very, very wrong.

It never occurred to me that things could get worse.

After we brought our sons home from the hospital, I had to handle them very gently at first. Neither child could hold his bottle or feed himself. Much like having twins, I had to juggle their feedings. Of course, Sonja could eat without assistance, thank God. She was also a good mother's little helper. She was another set of legs and hands. She was only three years old, yet she was very eager to help. Glenn and Tyrone continued to wear soft neck braces and pretty much just lie on their backs all day. I enjoyed dressing my children, combing their hair, and rubbing on all the sweet smelling lotions and powders for babies. Like powder, there was always a sprinkle of sadness over my happiness as I went about caring for them. We all seemed to have our own way of coping with it as a family.

My life had become so habitual and predictable without the spontaneity of fun or free time. Jacky worked all day and sometimes on the weekends. After dinner, he typically went out with the boys, my brother-in-law and cousin's husband. All of our free time together was spent with the kids. Jacky and I rarely went out together in our early years. I was a homebody, and I didn't want to leave my kids with anyone if I didn't have to because of their delicate condition.

While we had lost much of the intimacy we shared at the beginning of our relationship, Jacky and I were still very good parents and mates. We managed our household well and took very good care of our children. We did everything together as a family and enjoyed the family time, despite not having much time to ourselves as a couple. Jacky was an excellent provider and very conscientious about his responsibilities to his family. We had purchased our first new car, a green Volkswagen Beetle, shortly after Tyrone was born. It certainly was great having our own transportation for taking our children back and forth to doctor's appointments and for pleasure rides around the city mostly on the weekends.

Sonja busied herself in the back seat looking out the window or playing with a toy, while her little brother, Glenn, sat propped up next to her. I'm sure he liked watching his fussy sister. I held Tyrone on my lap up front. It was a tight fit, but we all enjoyed being in a car, not walking or catching the bus anymore; we rode along taking in the sights.

LIFE-THREATENING SURGERIES

Through the eyes of the public, everything appeared fine. We never expressed the emotional strain of having two helpless sons. It was our brand of a normal life. We didn't tell anyone or seek out anyone's help. We had too much pride. It prevented us from letting anyone know how difficult it was to handle our children's issues, so we handled them our way, the best we could. Of course, our families knew our sons weren't well, but we never showed them how much it was paining us on the inside caring for them. They never truly knew the full extent of what was going on; we just didn't talk about it.

I was certainly amiss about everything being fine. Glenn became progressively worse. He remained under-developed, not growing or behaving like other babies his age. He made funny bird-like sounds when he should have been forming baby talk words. This worried me a lot, but the doctors always ignored me or evaded my questions, stating that all babies develop differently. I discovered on my own that Glenn was all or partially deaf. I noticed he was never startled when I surprised him with a loud noise, even while he slept. And he didn't respond to my voice when I played with him. On purpose, I would try to make noises to scare him, but he never showed any reaction. I kept this to myself, hoping that I was wrong. When children can't hear, children can't speak. I didn't know that then, but that explained the bird sounds that Glenn made. His hearing wasn't addressed. I think other symptoms were more urgent and the doctors probably felt it could wait because his neck showed no improvement.

Glenn became thinner and thinner, appearing emaciated even though he ate reasonably well. You could feel and see the bones in his body. Eventually, he started having very large bowel movements inconsistent with his intake of food. It frightened me to death. My gut feeling was that he was wasting away. And, in a way, I was right. At a regular visit to the doctor, I was informed that the surgery did not achieve what it was supposed to achieve, and Glenn was surely going to die. Die! I was in shock. I can't remember saying or feeling anything after they said that word. It really cut deep and for a while I went completely numb. My head started spinning, my legs felt as if they were going to fold, and all the life in me seemed as if it was quickly draining out of me. I felt like I was dying myself. Somehow, some way I managed to leave the hospital. I don't know how I made it home with Glenn in my arms in the fragile condition I was in. Surely God was supporting me and helping me put one foot in front of the other. After I got there, I walked around my house totally confused, thinking this must be a dream; it can't be reality. I must have stared at Glenn for hours, soaking up every memory

LIFE-THREATENING SURGERIES

of him. He looked so innocent and sweet. Why was God going to let him die? I always hoped everything would be fine. How could God let me down? Was Glenn going to die that day? Next week? When? We had a special bond through our experiences. How could I let him go? It was difficult for me to understand why God turned His back on us. After all we had struggled through together, God was telling me no. I just couldn't imagine one day my baby would be gone, never to be seen or held again. How could my life go on without him? How could God let me down?

> *I always hoped everything would be fine. How could God let me down?*

I wanted so badly to break down in front of someone, but I still couldn't. At least, that's what I thought. I don't know why my heart wasn't willing to share pain with others; it yearned to, but something inside me made me hold on to it alone. It was an ever-so-growing inner battle to cry out for help; I held on to it so long it wouldn't come out even if I wanted it to. It kept building up more and more inside me until I thought my heart would burst. It is amazing how much pressure you train yourself to bear. Still, I'm sure no one suspected the amount of inner turmoil Jacky and I were going through. We continued to wear masks that didn't reflect our true selves. As usual, we acted as if everything was fine, attending family gatherings with smiles on our faces that never faltered.

If they believed anything differently, they didn't express it. As they say, it was "business as usual." It made sense. Our family, much like others during that period of time, was the kind of family that did not air our troubles in public unless it was absolutely necessary. Our families were always supportive and always there for each other, but we did not dare mention our inner turmoil. It was taboo to bring up what you were going through. So, I kept my pain between God and me. Anyway, I needed a miracle and only God could perform that.

Initially, I didn't even tell Jacky that Glenn was going to die. I just couldn't bring myself to do it. I didn't want him to be as devastated as I was. I'd never seen him fall apart, and I didn't want to either. Knowing Glenn was going to die left a knot in my stomach, which I carried around from that day on. I thought I was shielding Jacky from being tormented and that was my reason for not telling him. He needed peace of mind to work and provide for his family. I had matured during my short time as a mother, and I knew that wasn't the right thing to do. It was selfish of me and wasn't fair to Jacky or to our families.

LIFE-THREATENING SURGERIES

As the months went by, I became obsessed with the disease. Too many of my waking hours were devoted to searching for answers, but the disease is very rare, and therefore I couldn't find any answers. When doctors don't have answers, you really feel desperate and alone. Everyone depends on doctors to have the answers and give you some kind of explanation, but for my sons they didn't. Over the years, I've talked to several medical doctors and most of them never heard of Conradi's Disease. I had come to a brick wall; I couldn't get over it, around it, or through it.

SUICIDE VS. SALVATION

Feeling absolutely hopeless, suicidal thoughts started swirling around in my mind. It's not easy to admit publicly that I wanted to kill myself, even worse my two sons along with me. But it's true. Glenn's condition was a consuming fire that had raged out of control within my soul. I had slipped into a very, very dark hole. I didn't care about anything anymore. My burden felt like corked pressure ready to pop at any time. Finally, I was broken down. I didn't want to bear my burden any longer. For some reason, I felt a sense of ease or freedom transitioning from self-preservation to self-destruction. I guess self-preservation was too difficult and giving up seemed easier. I just wasn't happy anymore. I was simply spent, let down, and frantically needing physical and mental satisfaction. I was broken down from crying day in and day out. The salt from my tears even burned my face because my cheeks stayed irritated from wiping my eyes. Feeling despair, I decided I wanted a way out.

GRAIN OF HOPE

I thought of ways to kill myself until I finally came up with the plan that made the most sense at the time. The plan consisted of taking both of my sons in each arm and walking straight into one of the rivers nearby. My bizarre plan would solve all of our problems. Crippled by continuous blows to my emotions, I couldn't think straight, and I didn't care enough to think straight anymore. Nothing mattered. And besides, I thought Jacky and Sonja could live a more normal and better life without all of our problems. My sons would no longer have any more pain and suffering; all pain for our family would finally come to an end.

Mental darkness is an evil force that builds up for weeks and months or however long it takes until it eventually grabs hold of you to prevent your destiny and destroy you if you don't see a way to stop it. I was young and had been living in a nightmare for almost two years. After weeks of trying to find my way through the fog, I came up with what I thought was a good reason for suicide. What a brainstorm. I guess that's why they call it a storm.

By the grace of God and His divine enlightenment, Sonja saved my life, and I guess you could say Glenn and Tyrone's lives, too. The importance of my daughter's life shone like a bright light through the darkness of my mind. It gave me real purpose and the will to hold on to the remnants of my life. She was my light at the end of the tunnel that sent

SUICIDE VS. SALVATION

me back to this world. Sonja was my first child and the one who changed my life for the better and filled it with joy. She would never know how much I loved her. Sparing her life would not necessarily prove that I loved her; it would probably do the opposite. She may even grow up feeling like I chose to take my sons with me and leave her behind again. Could I dare leave her by suicide? It would be a stain she would wear the rest of her life. Besides, her birth made me a woman; she was the reason I married and a constant reminder of the beauty in our marriage. Even though Jacky could always get another wife, I wanted to be Sonja's only mom. I found a reason to live, a reason to struggle, and a reason to hope for change.

Besides, her birth made me a woman; she was the reason I married and a constant reminder of the beauty in our marriage.

In a state of utter confusion and weariness, God opened my eyes to understand and see how unconscionable it would be to leave Sonja without her mother, how selfish and uncaring I would be for not considering her needs as just as important as her brothers'. It was a hard lesson. Believing in God is not always easy; He performs His will in mysterious ways without our help. Once I stopped focusing on me, my thoughts shifted to another direction, and I was able to see the reality and the importance of all that I had in my life. There was still a future. I struggled, but overcame the feeling of self-pity. I stopped giving in to the negative thoughts that had plagued my mind. God used a firm hand, empowering me to take a firm stance in appreciating my life. I had a daughter, two sons, and a husband who loved me, and I loved them too. There was still tomorrow.

Everyone must find the most important reason to live, whether it is a thing or a person. I believe everyone has somebody who is near and dear to his or her heart. Cling on to them in a crisis; you will eventually realize they are your saving grace. You tend to forget them when your mind is so preoccupied and swept up in overwhelming circumstances. Remember how important your love is to them and how important their love is to you. Dig your heels in and don't let a crisis break up your family and splinter all of your dreams for the future. I thought I was solving one problem, but I was getting ready to create an even greater one. So, even though my life had become a bitter pill, I swallowed it and with a determination to live, ascended slowly out of that deep, dark hole I had desperately fallen into. I found joy: Sonja.

SUICIDE VS. SALVATION

So, even though my life had become a bitter pill, I swallowed it and with a determination to live, ascended slowly out of that deep, dark hole I had desperately fallen into.

You see, losing hope clouded all common sense and set the stage for dancing with death. But, remembering the reason to live made the difference between overcoming a problem versus being overcome by the problem. Life is always meaningful and purposeful to others and certainly to God. Others, because someone you may not necessarily know will need you in their life, and God, because you must never abort God's purpose of how and when He will use you. In time, you will learn that a crisis tries to shatter the hopes of a family, but if you prevail, it has an equal ability to strengthen and unite your family together in a bond of love for one another that endures forever.

We've seen this wonderful bonding occur in other cases, such as with the Kennedy family when President John F. Kennedy and his brother, Robert, were publicly murdered. It was very inspiring to watch their family support each other.

Why some people are tried at such high levels we will never know. I believe the higher or greater the trial, the greater God's love abounds, and the greater your thirst is to draw closer to Him or move further away from Him. I don't believe God causes a crisis. I do believe if you have one, He is able to rush in to save and empower you. Give Him the opportunity to show His glory by giving Him glory.

I don't believe God causes a crisis. I do believe if you have one, He is able to rush in to save and empower you.

I eventually told Jacky that Glenn was going to die. At first, it was inconceivable to him. The peace in his face soon turned to fear. It was such a shock. His eyes turned glassy as they slowly filled with tears. He didn't question the truth because it matched what he could see: Glenn showed no real signs of recovering or getting better. The memory of that day and how pitiful Jacky looked as he wrapped his arms around his firstborn son, sobbing while he pressed him lovingly against his chest, is burned into my brain. That momentous sight still pierces my heart whenever I reflect back on that day. Time was running out, and Jacky deserved and was entitled to share the short time he had left to release his emotions to his son. Letting Glenn go was going to be devastating. It was only fair that Jacky knew beforehand so that he could say his goodbyes, hold Glenn, and kiss him during his final moments. I told him that I had known for a while and of course he wanted to know why I didn't tell him. He wasn't annoyed by my answer; he always understood and trusted my reasons. As it turned out, it was better it happened this way. I could be more supportive for Jacky since I knew earlier and had become more at ease and somewhat prepared. I left Jacky alone with Glenn perched on his knee, sitting on the living room chair until he was ready to give him up for his nightly bath before bed. They stayed in there for a couple of hours before Jacky finally handed him over to me for bedtime.

A DAY AT THE PARK

As the days went by, Glenn continued to get weaker. At almost two years old, he never sat up straight or crawled. He was very small for his age, appearing to be eight months old. He never spoke words, just made funny sounds. His head was still wobbly. Basically, he had stopped developing, and the expression on his face showed that he was suffering. It was almost impossible to watch him deteriorate as the days went by. I knew it was time to let Glenn go. I prayed God would end his suffering and take him. My prayers changed from God please heal Glenn to God please stop the suffering, understanding that meant his death.

I prayed God would end his suffering and take him.

One hot summer day in June, I thought it would be a good idea to take the kids to the park for a breath of fresh air after Jacky arrived home from work. I had a basket packed and the kids were ready when Jacky walked in the door. The kids and I waited for him to change from work clothes to regular clothes. There were some really nice parks near our apartment. We all piled in the car and off to the park we went. We found a nice spot to spread a blanket and began to enjoy the day.

Your mind can play tricks on you under extreme stress. It seemed that as I laid Glenn down on the blanket, he appeared to start sinking below the ground. I can't say whether or not this was my imagination, some kind of sign, or my mind preparing me for what was to come. Maybe it was all three. I didn't say a word about what had happened; people would think I was crazy. I continued to go on with our picnic.

The picnic turned out to be a good idea. We had a great time. The children were very sleepy by the time we got home that evening. I didn't bother to bathe them, just wiped their faces, undressed them, and put them directly in bed. The fresh air caused them to fall off to sleep rather quickly.

Sonja slept in her bed in the same room with Glenn as he slept in her old crib. Tyrone, who was now only ten months old, slept on the couch in the living room. I had another trick of taking the pillows off the couch, propping

A DAY AT THE PARK

them against the open section of the couch, lining the open inner section with soft blankets and a sheet, and turning it into Tyrone's abode. Tyrone always slept with a pacifier in his mouth. Jacky and I put the kids to bed, and then we turned in early.

During the night, Tyrone started crying. His pacifier had fallen out of his mouth. I went into the living room to put the pacifier back in Tyrone's mouth. For no apparent reason, I felt something was strange as I sat there on the couch patting Tyrone's back and trying to get him to go back to sleep. Suddenly, a shadow appeared at the bottom of the apartment door. A light in the main hallway of our building stayed on all night. It was easy to see the shadow. It appeared like someone was standing at the door. Whoever it was never knocked, and then they walked away. It frightened me.

After Tyrone went calmly back to sleep, I got up from the couch and went back to my bed. It was habit for me to check in on the kids before going back to bed; that night I didn't. Something felt strange and I couldn't wait to get back to the comfort of my own bed next to Jacky. To my surprise, Sonja had gotten out of her bed and was snuggled up to her father sound sleep. I squeezed in next to her, then went back to sleep.

GRAIN OF HOPE

I was awakened early the next morning by Jacky's loud cries. I already knew why he was crying as soon as I heard him. He had found Glenn dead. I couldn't bear to go near the room; I didn't want to see Glenn's lifeless body. I called my mother and sister. I can't remember who called the police. When the police carried his body from the apartment, I went into the kitchen and turned my back so that I couldn't see them carry his tiny body from the house. It was just too awful for me to handle. It was reassuring that Jacky had not gone to work yet; he was there to do what I couldn't. Less than one month after letting Jacky know Glenn was going to die, Glenn died. I am so glad that I told him a few weeks before.

> *I was awakened early the next morning by Jacky's loud cries. I already knew why he was crying as soon as I heard him.*

Accepting that your loved one lost the battle of life is a bad reality. Getting to that stage of acceptance takes what seems like a lifetime because of a resistive desire not to say goodbye or let go. Your children are under your skin, and you can't shed them.

The next time I looked upon Glenn's face, he was lying in a small coffin at the local funeral home. Glenn had a small

A DAY AT THE PARK

funeral. After the ceremony, I affectionately embraced his coffin during the entire slow and winding road to his gravesite. We arrived at the cemetery, and everyone filed out of their cars. The coffin was gently taken out of the vehicle and carried over to a deep hole in the ground. I couldn't bear to watch him get lowered into a dark, deep hole in the ground, so I requested that he not be lowered until after I left. I remember getting back into the car, careful to avoid looking back at his little coffin sitting there next to its final destination as I rode away. I thought it best to forget all about Glenn and just walk away.

I never went back to that awful place. That day, a part of me went into the grave with him. I don't know why my initial reaction was to detach from Glenn, as if it were possible to forget an almost two-year battle to save his life like it had never happened. But, it did happen, and I couldn't escape the entire experience. It haunted me day and night for many years.

I mourned Glenn more as the days went by. I missed my little fellow and mourning him seemed endless. I couldn't forget him. What was my life going to be like without Glenn? My heart was wounded and empty from the void created by his death. For days, I would stare endlessly into the heavens, imagining that he was floating amongst the clouds somewhere. I was always hoping that I would see his tiny face peering down at me from behind a cloud. It is the missing that is more painful than the shock of the death. Mothers in the family set the standard and leadership of how the family and others respond to emotional situations. If I hold my head up high, then others will too; it can be the opposite as well. But, my head was held high. They were all right because I was all right. My family understood Glenn's prognosis and at that time, death was a mystery, a scary subject that people avoided talking about. In the African American culture, we celebrate a Christian's death as a home going. We believe they are spiritually alive in the presence of God. Something we all look forward to. Death is a reality we live with each day. I still miss Glenn and imagine what he would be like if he were still alive today. Glenn died June 10, 1970. Before I die, I want to go back where I left him and place flowers on his grave.

STARTING AGAIN

A mother's strength holds the whole family together. When she weakens, everyone in the family tends to weaken, and the family structure is left in shambles. We were all handicapped, and in some ways, we all died with Glenn in our own way. The personal guilt as parents is shameful. Though I didn't show it, everything that was going on in my life ate away at me on the inside. On the outside I was perfectly composed, while on the inside I was empty, the pain of losing one child and the looming dark cloud of Tyrone's diagnosis confronting me head on, twisting and tormenting my mind day and night. Our lives constantly unraveled and frayed like snags in a fine knit sweater. The battle to save our children started taking an emotional toll on our family, its victims.

Jacky buried himself in his work at the plant, working overtime. He stopped going to functions and family gatherings with me. Sonja was increasingly deprived of attention. She said to me one day, "Ma, I wish I was handicapped too." That's as bad as it gets. In a crisis, everyone's feelings are important, even if you don't personally agree or emotionally feel the connection or same sense of urgency as someone else. In a crisis, people and family that are important to you sometimes become invisible. Those closest to us are often the ones who suffer the most when we can't give them what they need. We assume they understand. Children often lack the maturity to understand what the mature griever is personally going through. It is crucial that mature grievers try to keep their hearts objective and eyes and ears open. Is it easy? No, it most certainly is not. I think it takes perseverance to be rational in a crisis. Yet even though it seems impossible, it is always very important to force yourself to stay open-minded.

For many years, I was accustomed to living with hurt. It was natural, as normal and automatic as breathing. But that didn't make it easy. That's the thing about pain. Like many difficult emotions, once you have adjusted to them, they have such permanency. You can live with pain a long time but the longer you bear it the more it becomes unbearable. It will cause you to drop to your knees. I spent many nights and days on my knees and it's safe to say I was tired of living in pain.

We were traumatized by Glenn's death. We had fractured lives, not knowing or understanding what each other needed to become whole again. I am ashamed to say that we were not aware of social programs or support groups that aided families. Jacky and I were both raised to make the best of life. The old pull yourself up by your bootstraps was the adage of the day and probably still stands in traditional families. It wasn't polite to talk about your personal problems openly, an unwritten rule carried over from childhood. Problems are to be confined within the four walls of your house. And sometimes, within the confines of your own mind. You just sort of went about working with what you had and tried to be satisfied with that. We didn't plan for our lives to spin out of control, it just happened. We wanted so badly to live our lives like most people, and we were forced to find our new normal.

We continued our fight to beat the odds for Tyrone. And we did. Or at least, we tried to. I completely ignored his prognosis. I was not going to go through this nightmare again. I took Tyrone on as my personal mission, a special task God had presented just for me. I wanted to prove the medical community wrong, and I was bound and determined to do it. After all, doctors can be wrong. I was obsessed; death was not going to win. When you think about it, there's as much chance for something to go right as there is for something to go wrong. So why not hope? Why not continue to live as if Tyrone would surpass doctors' expectations? There was no other option.

MOVING ON AND AWAY

Several months after Glenn's death, we moved away. It was difficult to live in the same house where our son died. My mother told me about some new townhouses recently built in a nearby suburb right outside of the city. Sonja was almost four years old and would be starting kindergarten soon, and Tyrone was one year old.

As the cliché goes, it was a fresh start for us, "adjusting" emotionally and physically to a new environment. "Adjusting" is just a word I am using but it was not a possibility in our real life. A child missing out of the family is not like dropping off clothes you can't fit at Goodwill. It is not like getting rid of an old piece of furniture you had enjoyed sitting in for years that became worn down, stained and ugly. These are things you loved and are forced to do without. Children do not fit in these categories. You can't "adjust" to the loss of a child. I can't think of a word to describe the empty space I carried in my soul where Glenn belonged. He was a missing piece of our family puzzle; only his size and shape could fit in order to complete the puzzle. He left a void I carried with me everywhere and at all times. There was no adjusting.

I can't think of a word to describe the empty space I carried in my soul where Glenn belonged.

Our new home was on Glenn Avenue, now isn't that ironic? The townhouse was much nicer and roomier than our living space in the Projects. I was glad we made the switch to a safer, residential neighborhood. The townhouse had a second floor, three bedrooms, a basement, and our own private backyard for our children to enjoy. I always had an eye for design and our townhouse was very tastefully decorated. We installed beautiful wall-to-wall royal blue carpet throughout the second-floor bedrooms and a Parisian sunset shag carpet on the main floor. We had a beautiful celery green sofa covered with a satin on chenille-striped fabric, and we hung matching draperies. We proudly displayed family pictures. Most every morning I propped up Tyrone against the corner of the couch as he and Sonja sat transfixed by the TV screen showing Mister Rogers' Neighborhood and Sesame Street. We only had channels 2, 4, and 11; cable wasn't yet available. Morgan Freeman was part of the cast of Sesame Street, not yet the award-winning movie star we know today.

MOVING ON AND AWAY

We needed a change of scenery, so we purchased new furniture too. Sonja had a mint green French provincial dresser, perfect for a young girl. She often felt neglected, but we tried to make sure she had the best and lived the most comfortable life possible given the circumstances. Jacky and I also purchased a new dresser and a chest of drawers. Sonja and Tyrone had teak-stained bunk beds; as children, they were kept close. There would no longer be a need to sleep in a dresser drawer or inside the open pillow-less section in a couch.

It was enjoyable to decorate our new house. We needed a change and a diversion of any kind. The new house brightened and lifted our spirits and gave us plenty of much-needed space and comfort. It helped us move away from painful memories. It was a new start to help in overcoming some grief. Our home showed all the beauty of a wonderful life, but nothing could beautify the unhappiness that resided in our hearts from the death of Glenn. The pain hadn't left us. Glenn's death was a permanent scar, though we hid it. We tried to make life great; we made every effort to one day make it as great as we hoped it would become.

On weekends we continued to go on family rides in our little green Volkswagen Beetle. Life was full of simple pleasures. In the back of our minds we knew that Tyrone's life could be taken away in an instant, so we didn't take anything for granted and we didn't stress over minor incidents that send some families over the edge. I guess you could say we didn't cry over spilled milk. We stuck together, strengthened by our crisis rather than being torn apart. Grieving Glenn's death was fresh in our minds and hearts, and with Tyrone's health up in the air, any straying from Jacky or Sonja would have sent me over the edge again. Their quiet support helped me continue each day, containing my pain and plastering a smile on my face. We had a steady income, a nice home, and a car, so people assumed we were doing well; on the surface it appeared we were. It would be a mistake to expect that our material progress made us totally happy. Little did people know the pain and sadness we were harboring within the four walls of our home every day.

I guess you could say we didn't cry over spilled milk. We stuck together, strengthened by our crisis rather than being torn apart.

We arose from sleep each morning and prepared for the day like most families. For the most part, when we didn't think about it, we were happy and complete. I typically fed and watched Tyrone and Jacky attended to

MOVING ON AND AWAY

Sonja most of the time. Days were simple; we entertained ourselves around television, family birthdays, holiday celebrations, and the occasional family vacation. It goes without saying that we were in church every Sunday thanking God for His blessings.

Despite our beautiful new home, we were still missing a precious member of our family. Our new home was absent of Glenn's gentle presence. We went about living our lives grieving Glenn and fearing Tyrone's prognosis. Of course, Tyrone and Sonja were not aware of Tyrone's glum future. Tyrone believed and expected that one day he would walk and become like other children. What was wrong with believing that? He was happy and healthy and doing okay. He already lived beyond six months, so what did the doctors really know? As time went on we stopped living in fear that Tyrone would die at any moment. Instead, it was more positive to keep hoping and believing that Tyrone would, at best, prove the doctors wrong. If the doctors couldn't find answers about the disease, then what were we to know? After Tyrone passed the nineteenth-month mark, we weren't going to live with the message, "Tyrone has six months to live" in our heads any longer.

PATRICK

To my surprise, two years after moving into our new home, I was pregnant again for the fourth time. We were happy to have another child, but a bit apprehensive too. Surely, this child would be a normal baby. I prayed it would be a normal baby. It had to be. I didn't know what I would do if it wasn't. Again, in my arms I carried a small two-year-old child and in my belly a growing baby. However, there were two major differences from before: I didn't have to travel back and forth to a clinic with Tyrone every month as I did with Glenn. I also had a car at my disposal. For the most part, the pregnancy didn't cause me any additional discomfort. I went to my usual check-ups and everything was progressing as it should be.

One early morning, nine months later, my water broke. Jacky was at work and Sonja was in school. Luckily, my uncle was visiting that morning (probably trying to get a free breakfast). Little did he know he was about to be put to work. My uncle handled everything; he got me to the hospital and Tyrone to one of my sisters' houses. I had an exceptional family of devoted uncles, nieces, and nephews who loved and provided support when and wherever needed. I was grateful he was there that morning. I can't imagine trying to strap Tyrone into his seat in the car and then getting to the hospital while in labor.

I had an exceptional family of devoted uncles, nieces, and nephews who loved and provided support when and wherever needed.

After an easy labor, the delivery turned out to be devastating; the baby died. We named him Patrick. The hospital staff never brought Patrick to me. I didn't get the chance to hold him in my arms. We were told he died of a hole in his heart and I'm sure there were other complications of Conradi's Disease. Patrick was taken away and buried at the foot of an unknown person, where and when, we were never told. After carrying him all those months, I left the hospital empty-handed and spiritually empty. I missed the experience of the soft touch of my new baby, the cry of his tiny voice, and his sweet baby smell. I can't remember much about that day, probably because of the shock of it all. I do remember waking up the next day and looking over at my obstetrician who was quietly sitting with his head down in a chair in the corner of my room. With a solemn look on his face like I had never seen

PATRICK

in him, he offered his condolences and tried to comfort me. I had experienced doctors in the past that were less pleasant and caring than I had desired, so this was an entirely new and refreshing experience. Nowadays, doctors undergo some sort of sensitivity training at the very least. They learn how to talk to patients, how to listen. Most of them don't appear as insensitive as the doctors were when my children were babies. Another sign of the changing times, I suppose.

Jacky was not at my bedside when I woke. I knew he was spiritually broken, void of feelings, and unable to face me. It was probably for the best. He did come to bring me home from the hospital though. I was ashamed and completely disappointed. To be full of excitement for nine months, anxiously anticipating a new baby, making preparations and plans, only to leave the hospital with nothing but an empty belly and empty arms void of a warm, happy baby didn't feel real. What would we tell our families? Our friends? Sonja? I felt like a failure—as a mother, as a parent. This pregnancy was supposed to impart hope and joy into our lives. But in an instant, our anticipated joy was taken away, our grain of hope a speck blowing away in the wind. We were silent as Jacky pushed me in a wheelchair down the long hallway onto the elevator to get down to the front door of the hospital. I felt

GRAIN OF HOPE

so cheated watching happy mothers get helped into their cars as they carefully carried their new bundles of joy. Something that was supposed to be an exciting and proud moment for us turned out to be humiliating and we hung our heads in sorrow. How did we ever keep functioning? The only explanation had to be through the power of God.

This pregnancy was supposed to impart hope and joy into our lives. But in an instant, our anticipated joy was taken away, our grain of hope a speck blowing away in the wind.

Part 2

GROWING OUR FAMILY

Patrick's birth and death happened so suddenly. It was surreal and numbing like, "What just happened in our lives again?" It was a crushing blow to two already heavy hearts. But I had two children who needed me; again, I had to get it together. I didn't know how I would, but I trusted God and desperately hoped He would show me the way. I'm sure Jacky talked everything over with our families and probably told Sonja a little girl-like story of why mommy didn't bring home a baby. I was in such a state of shock that I'm not entirely sure how everyone else heard the news. No one ever mentioned it to me, and for that I was grateful. Our children were protected because they were too young to understand the constant disasters occurring all around them. Jacky and I were just bewildered; we'd been longing to welcome a healthy baby boy into the family. Sonja's little mind was probably hoping to see her new brother, but she didn't feel the pain because of her tender age.

The following year, I became pregnant for the fifth time. We wanted a larger family, so we didn't give up, but maybe we should have. In retrospect, I would have. Young and naïve can be a formula for mistakes at times, but was there really anything wrong with wanting a large family? Pregnancy symbolizes nature's miraculous blossoming of new life, new beginnings, and a new day. It is the feeling of the sun rising within your body with the glow of a bright sunny day. Yet in a moment, the sun set in mine, casting a shadow over my soul because the womb that provided the promise of a new life became a still, dark grave deep within.

Five months into the pregnancy, I called my doctor to let him know that my baby died. He was amazed that I knew there was a difference in feeling pregnant or not. He said most women cannot tell the difference, but I did. I knew I was walking around during the day and sleeping during the night with my dead baby entombed inside me. My doctor made arrangements for me to come to the office in order to confirm what I already knew. And, I was right. My five-month-old baby boy was removed from my body and all that remained was the feeling of emptiness and sorrow that I felt again and again. Death was becoming a normal part of our lives. I wasn't given an opportunity to see my little boy, our baby boy Williams. There was no bonding, just a cold sterile procedure and a release from the hospital.

I hated myself. After arriving back home, I looked in the mirror and began randomly cutting plugs of hair out of my head. It seemed like a good way to punish the face that stared back at me. Afterwards, I slowly dropped to the bathroom floor, sobbing because of what I had done. I still had to be a wife and I still had to be a mother. I buried my feelings and did what I had to do. In-between pregnancies and deaths, I had to continue on. Thankfully, I had Tyrone to keep me company throughout the day. He was my adorable little buddy—my constant, adoring companion.

> *In-between pregnancies and deaths, I had to continue on.*

After Sonja went to school and Jacky to work, it was just Tyrone and me left home alone. There were no options for daycare, and he was much too complicated for family members to care for. My day was like most stay-at-home moms. I got busy making beds, cleaning the bathroom, and coming up with a meal for dinner each evening. Tyrone was no bother because, for the most part, I just put him where I wanted him to be and he stayed there until I was ready to move him, always where he could see me. He was in his own little world and not responsive to mine. He wasn't stimulated by anything, just sort of laid there with unfocused eyes and a sense of nobody being inside his small, rigid body. But I knew he was there. I could feel his loving little soul. We moved around the house together pretty much doing the same thing every day. Tyrone's place in the family was more like having a constant baby or young toddler in the home with the exception of the pitter-patter of little feet, getting into places he shouldn't be, breaking stuff, and falling. His quiet world was much different than Sonja's active one.

METAMORPHOSIS: FROM CATERPILLAR TO BUTTERFLY

Tyrone was about three years old when the doctors recommended he receive rehabilitation services. Since birth, Tyrone's body had been rigid to the point where we had to pry open his fingers. His arms were always held tight to his body as he laid there, eyes unfocused, pacifier in his mouth. It was good news to think Tyrone could possibly get some help. We were referred to a local children's hospital with a rehabilitation facility. It was located a few communities away from where we lived. There were many children; some lived there, while others visited daily to receive services. Many of the children there were like Tyrone, struggling to overcome all types of handicaps. Some children had only physical problems and others had both physical and mental challenges. The staff worked one-on-one with each child, striving diligently to reform and rehabilitate stubborn, resistant limbs and bodies, and indistinct minds.

I was familiar with clinics and hospitals, but this one was very unusual. I was overjoyed thinking that these people had the means to undo the tight wrapping of Tyrone's rigid and spastic body. I didn't know what physical therapy was. So even though I was leery, I wanted to believe that they could set him free. Up until that point, I didn't know if there was ever going to be a change in his condition. Of course, after being introduced to solid foods he could eventually control his tongue and he no longer cried all the time, but those changes were to be expected. Like most babies, he gradually changed too. But, we still felt like we were at a dead end. I thought everyone in the medical world was waiting around for him to die. After three years of doing nothing, somewhat miraculously, doctors finally believed Tyrone had hope. It was such a feeling of relief—one we always craved. My little buddy, the boy who I watched grow and improve in only very small ways, was going to get help with the mobility of this body in which he was trapped.

I continued taking Tyrone back and forth to doctor's appointments and physical therapy to help with his spasticity. Many of Tyrone's developmental years were spent in hospitals and clinics. Back then, medical institutions were cold and clinical and didn't include much coziness and fun. But we were being offered some

METAMORPHOSIS: FROM CATERPILLAR TO BUTTERFLY

help and much-needed encouragement for a change and we gladly accepted it. At the rehab facility, Tyrone had an assortment of doctors and staff. They were determined to mold and shape children with disabilities into able-bodied people or at least give them as much of a chance as possible to interact with the world around them. Tyrone was being offered a chance at a better future. Yes, future. Someone other than us was thinking he had a better life ahead of him. After having doctors only speak of his ominous fate, we were ecstatic to see this opportunity for Tyrone to live. One of the beauties of being young is that you have a lifetime to overcome or correct a bumpy start. During the day, Tyrone and I traveled back and forth to the rehab facility while Sonja was in school. My friends who lived next door or down the street were backup babysitters for Sonja in an emergency. This wasn't ideal for poor little Sonja, but it was what we had to do for the family at the time.

One of the beauties of being young is that you have a lifetime to overcome or correct a bumpy start.

The staff and I were happy with even the slightest changes Tyrone made. I admired their patience and persistence in the way they worked with the kids. It is not easy work. Sometimes they put forth a lot of effort to get little or no results. I'm sure Tyrone would not have been able to attend school or gain any of the major bodily motor skills that he achieved if it were not for their help. Through diligent and dedicated work, slowly but surely his team of therapists was able to peel away the little fellow's physical restraints and release to us a little boy that had a somewhat regular body with boundless potential. He overcame his rigidity and spasticity because of them. Tyrone became a new person. Over several years of intense therapy, they created a real wonder. Giving him credit too, Tyrone was a good worker; the more he endured, the greater his spirit thrived and the more vocal and alert he became. He was a willing participant in his metamorphosis, impressing and inspiring everyone around him. Even though he was a child, children and adults alike admired and loved him as he did them. He appeared to be a sprinter in an exhausting race, determined to cross the finish line. He had hope. It was written on his face and everyone was inspired by his bright, shining example of courage.

There was certainly something Godly in this special little boy. His sense of God was uncanny. At such a young age, he knew God. He spoke often of God in terms of a friend, trusting and believing that God could perform a miracle that would cause him to overcome his handicap and walk one day. His favorite scripture was Philippians 4:13, which states: "I can do all things through Christ which strengtheneth me" (KJV). He truly lived by those words. It fortified his hope for today and promise of tomorrow. We welcomed the power of God in our home; we needed Him so much. My family marched behind the banner I carried for God. This was important for us. While Glenn was sick, I felt like God had abandoned my prayers and my faith slipped. But, we were past those dark times and the small hope I started out with by now had flourished into a mighty faith.

He spoke often of God in terms of a friend, trusting and believing that God could perform a miracle that would cause him to overcome his handicap and walk one day.

I always believed that Tyrone would be like most children someday. He progressed for several years, slowly, moving upward and improving in his development. We met the challenging complications of his handicap as they emerged. I was convinced in my heart that God could do anything. Tyrone believed in me, and I believed in God; together we were looking forward to the day he would walk and become like other children. We always marched on, trying to keep our family strong and happy. We had a new house in a quaint neighborhood. Yes, we had lost babies and our beautiful boy, Glenn, but we still pulled together, laughed together, and made a life for ourselves. Tyrone's problems were our centermost concern in terms of medical care, and Sonja continued to be our little independent ray of light. Life was somewhat calm and normal. Well, as normal as it could be for a family in our situation. In reflection, I can see all the beauty and all the simple moments that I loved at the time and now cherish in my memories. We functioned as any loving family would, albeit under the umbrella of impending future medical issues and problems similar to Glenn's.

Around the age of four, Tyrone still only made funny sounds and could not formulate words. At first, we attributed this to the disease. However, to make sure, we were referred to a Mental Health/Mental Retardation (MH/MR) facility for observation and testing. The MH/MR facility worked in conjunction with the physical therapy team at the rehab facility to find out the degree of his mental capabilities. The professionals there were like archaeologists, excavating and uncovering the mysteries in his mind. They discovered that Tyrone's vision was greatly impaired and so was his hearing. We learned that if you can't hear, you can't talk. If you can't see well, you can't identify most things around you. After fitting him with a hearing aid and eyeglasses, and undergoing one minor eye surgery, the world that was a blur suddenly popped open. Now he was eager to learn and get involved with his new world. He was adorable and content in his "Coke-bottle glasses" wearing his hearing aid.

The professionals there were like archaeologists, excavating and uncovering the mysteries in his mind.

While Tyrone spent his days at the rehab facility, Sonja loved going to school. She was learning new things like her shapes, colors, alphabets, and numbers. She was at the age where you make friends and fumble around in your own little world. Tyrone's world was much different than Sonja's. A day for him was not interacting with other children like Sonja, but having one-on-one speech and language therapies and pediatric rehabilitation by uniformed professionals. We helped him with his academic development in-between physical therapy and doctor's appointments in the same manner as we did Sonja. For the most part, it seemed that he was not ready for the academics we hoped he'd be ready for. Jacky and I encouraged learning his alphabet, numbers, and object identification through playtime interaction. But for him, it seemed it was most important to overcome multiple physical conditions so that he could one day possibly attend school just like Sonja. He didn't have to worry about making friends on the playground or staying in the lines when coloring. Because Tyrone didn't know any different since his disability had existed since birth, he didn't compare himself or feel jealousy toward Sonja and her exciting new childhood experiences. He had more challenges to overcome, so comparisons were never the issue. For this I was grateful.

Tyrone endured about five years of intense therapies to complete the metamorphosis. He was like the sluggish caterpillar that has to shed its rigid outer skin to grow into a beautiful butterfly, setting itself free to experience the world. Before he left the doctors at the rehab facility, he could sit in a special corner seat alone, stand in locked braces, and had acquired the agility of his fingers and hands. Overall, Tyrone had twelve minor surgeries—one to correct crossed eyes and eleven to relieve spasticity and tight joints. After it was all over, our little man could hold his own fork and spoon to feed himself and drink independently from a cup. Any mother can appreciate the feeling of a child's independence and the freedom given to her. Nothing was greater than hearing him verbalize

METAMORPHOSIS: FROM CATERPILLAR TO BUTTERFLY

words to form sentences. After waiting so many years, the funny sounds had vanished and we could communicate with each other. He made tremendous leaps and bounds in his progress.

Suddenly, Tyrone was not that same somber baby-like fellow I had been carrying around from room to room anymore. Though he didn't attend school because of his physical limitations until he was about seven years old, his mind certainly grew sharper as time passed. He became an animated Curious George-like character. He soaked up knowledge like a sponge. I couldn't help but wonder: Was he thinking and wondering all those years but couldn't get it out? He learned to ask questions and understand answers, finally making him a participating contributor to the family. Even though it was a little fuzzy for a while, we were gradually able to understand him in the same manner that we had used to understand Sonja. It takes patience and compassion helping a child grow and learn words. It was so sweet to witness him learning to talk and make gestures. It was fascinating to see his body break through the rigidity and spasticity that had bound him for so many years. It was a miracle. Envisioning the day that Tyrone was not going to be left out of life anymore left a happy feeling in our hearts. Both mind and body were delivered out of a lull to an awakening.

Though he didn't gain the strength and neurological ability to stand on his own two feet and take a step, he stood tall in character and spirit. He was provided a wheelchair—something I hated even though it was very helpful. For me, its presence solidified that he was not going to walk any time soon, though it did give him the mobility and ability to explore, both of which he did not have previously. It wasn't until around this time that Tyrone showed any emotions about his situation. He cried out to me one day, "Why can't I walk like other kids in the family?" My heart broke for him that day. I had no answer; I could only assure him that one day he would. But despite his wheelchair and his limitations, Tyrone was still my energetic little man.

BRIGHT BEGINNINGS

We moved to a ranch-style home that would accommodate a wheelchair, as well as make it easier to handle Tyrone. Sonja was ten by now and Tyrone seven. Tyrone was still stuck with me most of the time. Sonja always had the freedom to move about as she pleased. When she started her new school, she made friends right away and participated in activities like most kids. Tyrone enjoyed watching me do things around the house and playing on the porch with his friends. The only world he knew was experienced from a wheelchair.

We couldn't have asked for a better neighborhood. It had children the same ages as both Sonja and Tyrone, perfect for both of my kids. The street was a cul-de-sac, another great feature of the neighborhood. Sonja played and walked to school most days with the girls her age, while Tyrone had four regular friends. They played with him outside almost every day when the weather was nice. The winter months created more of a challenge. But most times, the kids' parents let them play inside with Tyrone. It probably gave the parents a little break. We always bought plenty of toys to attract kids. It was funny—the kids fought over Tyrone's toys and sometimes I would hear Tyrone fussing at them to break them up. The kids in the neighborhood were drawn to his magnetic personality. He was a real humdinger, this interesting character in a wheelchair. It overjoyed me to know that Tyrone had friends. Sometimes even Sonja's friends would wheel Tyrone up or down the street to their houses because they loved him too. For a long time, I worried that kids his age wouldn't accept him for the things that made him look different. Kids can be so cruel. But thank the Lord above, He blessed us with a kind neighborhood with kind individuals. Of course, some of the children stared at him at first, probably because they had never seen a wheelchair or didn't understand why their playmate got around in one. However, it was outrageous to see adults stare in the same manner. Stares were always embarrassing to Tyrone and to us. It was the only time that we felt different than—or maybe less than—other people. Thankfully, it was always a fleeting moment and we didn't internalize it too long. We, along with his extended family, always treated Tyrone like a normal child. And why not? He was normal to us.

As often as we could, we invited the kids in the neighborhood to gather at our house for playtime. One of the kids' favorite toys enjoyed was a carpenter set. We also went one step further by supplying the little carpenters real wood. They hammered, banged, and sawed what seemed like all day. I was glad to hear Tyrone having fun. However, my most vivid nightmare of fun I will never forget is when Jacky made Tyrone a go-cart. With his back bent forward, he would slowly push Tyrone to the top of the street. Once reaching the top, he would turn the go-cart around, facing the decline of about half a city block, and let it go. Tyrone flew down the street, feet strapped to fast moving pedals and hands to the handlebars. I wasn't home when he made this great invention, and rather discovered it the hard way.

One day as I got off the bus after finishing work, I turned on our street and there was Tyrone zooming down the middle of the street in his homemade go-cart with the biggest smile of excitement on his face from the thrill of the ride. I was so overwhelmed by fear that I couldn't speak. I had to call my mother to have her speak to Jacky because I wanted to choke him and I knew I would say all the wrong things. Men. All I could imagine was Tyrone sliding under an oncoming car turning onto the street, unaware of Tyrone, the disabled race car driver that had no ability or reflexes to move out of the way. What was Jacky thinking? Or rather, not thinking? I sympathized with him afterwards. I knew how badly he yearned for his son to be like other boys. He always used creativity to improvise and build toys so that Tyrone could have fun, too. It made me love him even more, seeing him try so hard to give our son a "normal" life.

Tyrone's cousins improvised and modified games and activities to include him in their fun too. Like the time they played baseball and pushed his wheelchair around the bases after he hit the ball. Or, they would swirl him around in his wheelchair to the music as a way of letting him dance. Tyrone acted like a "cool kid" and had a lot of rhythm as he bopped his head and swiveled his shoulders to the beat of the music.

It was always sad for us when Tyrone could not be included because of his limitations. I think because Tyrone was handicapped from birth it was not as crushing as if he had become disabled in an accident. He was used to his limitations and we sort of got used to them, too. I think his imagination helped keep his state of mind intact. Similar to watching celebrities, you know you'll never be one, but you love watching their lives anyway. I think we had a profound way of staying positive and realizing things could have been worse.

SCHOOL AND WORK BOUND

While in his earlier years he had to spend most of his day in physical therapy, the rehab facility's prosthetic department constructed the necessary adaptive equipment and devices to enable him to attend school. He could sit alone and stand in leg braces on a custom-made, wooden platform and board the wheelchair-accommodated school bus. Tyrone attended a special education school from elementary grades through senior high. It was an isolated, suburban school for children with special needs. Every child was given an IEP (Individual Education Plan) conference to assure each child received a customized education. The school was bright and stimulating, but it isolated children from the general population. We always tried so hard to include Tyrone and not segregate him, but this was prior to The Americans with Disabilities Act (ADA) when people with handicaps had a more difficult time navigating places. I didn't particularly want him to go there, but it was just another reality I learned to accept.

But what a relief! Sonja was in school and, at last, Tyrone was in school too. Jacky always worked, and shortly after Tyrone started school, I went to work for a utility company as a human resources clerk. Life gave me a time-out and I took it. All was good. We were finding our sense of normalcy under abnormal conditions. I believe God gave me extraordinary insight during this time of struggle, pain, and grief. I was not able to live a regular family life like most because Tyrone was not mobile and society had not progressed enough to accommodate—and in some cases, accept—an unusual family. I take no credit for all the wisdom I had to create normalcy and enhance the lives of our small family. I believe God's love for us guided us, His love imparting comfort and peace during every storm. Our family personified the scripture, "When you walk through the fire, you will not be burned; the flames will not set you ablaze" (Isaiah 43:2, NIV). Can you continue to live a good life in the face of pain and grief? Yes, you certainly can. A crisis is one part of your life, but not all of your life. Jacky and I worked, continuing to improvise and adjust to give our children the same kinds of social experiences and family life as any other parent under different circumstances would. The basic struggle in a crisis or tragedy is trying to find a sense of normalcy again.

SCHOOL AND WORK BOUND

Can you continue to live a good life in the face of pain and grief? Yes, you certainly can. A crisis is one part of your life, but not all of your life.

Probably up until Sonja was thirteen years old, Jacky worked night shift so it would allow him to be home with the kids when they came home from school until I got off work. The only problem was, we were not there for each other most of the time. Life is about making sacrifices, sacrifices, sacrifices. Every morning we strapped Tyrone in his braces, dressed him, fed him breakfast, wheeled him onto the school bus, and then off he went to school like any other kid. While we had to work hard and sacrifice to see one another, to give Tyrone and Sonja that normalcy of a regular school day and that great brother/sister interaction, Jacky and I were happy to oblige. Fortunately, at around the age of fourteen, Sonja became his primary babysitter, watching him until I got home from work and sometimes when Jacky and I were out for the evening. I paid teenagers in the neighborhood to watch Tyrone, too. It was nice to have the babysitters, as it freed us up for private time for ourselves. We were able to enjoy shopping at the malls and fun evenings out for dinner.

Working in corporate America opened the world to me and changed my life and children. Up until I started to work, my world was limited to just my family and our culture. I'm sure getting married at eighteen, and then having a baby at nineteen, stunted some of my development. After working at the utility company for some time, I left my position there for a job at a new company. I had to keep on living even though my circumstances weren't the best, and that meant going to work every day to maintain a regular working woman's life. There was the constant worry about Tyrone, and I hadn't forgotten about Glenn and the piece of me that had died with him. Joi, my new boss, exposed me to a whole new and different experience—one that I didn't know existed. I can never thank her enough for taking me under her wing and helping me to develop and grow when I wasn't aware that I needed to—what a kind young woman.

She helped me understand that even under stress and during unfortunate life circumstances, you have to fight for happiness. Untethered and free from the constraints of constant worry, Joi insisted on treating me to high-end restaurants, gourmet foods, boating excursions, and something very foreign to me, oysters on the half shell. I remember thinking that upper class people had such a wide scope of the world and the camaraderie and comfortableness to experience it. And in comparison, I felt that I had such a narrow view of many things. We were doing well financially, and I wanted my family to experience the same excitement that was out there for other people.

She helped me understand that even under stress and during unfortunate life circumstances, you have to fight for happiness.

In addition to eating "soul food," I wanted to broaden my understanding of the world, learning to prepare foods from other cultures as a means of exploration and growth. It was impossible to exclude the tasty flavors of soul food from our diets; I just included many other flavors as well, and my family thoroughly enjoyed the varieties offered by other cultures. Tyrone's favorite food, liver and gravy, was swapped with crab legs dipped in a melted butter and lemon juice combination. Sonja is still quite partial to sushi and exotic foods. We all enjoyed experiencing new things and broadening our horizons over a delicious plate of food.

We were "clothies" and "foodies." Weekly trips to the mall or boutique were our favorite activities. All of us were very well-dressed. We didn't have habits of using alcohol, cigarettes, or drugs. In contrast, a nice steak and lobster dinner was at the top of our list. We kept these two feasts in our home refrigerator in the same way that we kept ground beef and wieners. Food truly brought diversity into our home and lives. Back then, it gave us some unity and happiness, while also expanding our world right at our kitchen table. Eating at our house was like eating at a restaurant. This was especially important because Tyrone wasn't able to leave the house much; he had to experience most things from the comfort of our home. So to welcome change and liven up our lives, I learned to look beyond what I was accustomed to and comfortable with doing. Even to this day, it keeps my life interesting and active.

EBBS AND FLOWS

Life had become a series of ebbs and flows for us. While we had found a way to be happy as a family, we were still hurting. Just when it seemed like everything was on the right track, Tyrone had another setback. Because he had a late start in school and was academically delayed by at least three years, he was categorized as retarded. Being categorized as retarded turned out to be not all that bad; it afforded him more assistance and financial support for services, which proved to be very beneficial. Yet, it was on his personal records and files, creating another reason to be stigmatized. Other "normal" children his age didn't have the limitations he had. Still, Tyrone was capable of greatness and success; he wasn't hopeless. Unfortunately, for about a year I had to fight for Tyrone to be placed in a classroom with verbal children because he was improperly placed with non-verbal children at first. This is not a good placement for hearing impaired children. You see, I knew that he would improve if he could socialize with kids who could talk and interact with him because he picked up a lot at home listening to other kids, interacting with the family at dinner, and playing with others in the neighborhood. It was a hurdle, but we broke through, accustomed to so many ups and downs. It is large things like this that are small things to most people.

Many of the children at the school had multiple sclerosis and other disabilities that caused them to twitch or make floppy faces. For a while, I noticed Tyrone doing the same thing. At first, I thought it was one of the complications of Conradi-Hunermann syndrome. Then, one day, I happened to be watching something on TV where I learned that a kid was imitating another kid that had a physical twitch or something similar. I suspected Tyrone was doing the same thing. I immediately demanded Tyrone to STOP twitching. Eventually, he did. We were very fortunate because we really liked Tyrone's teachers and they loved him, but incidences like this one were a concern I had with special education. With each child having a different diagnosis, were they always going to be able to give my son the attention he needed? That's why we always found it important to have constant family involvement, especially when it came to education. Just as I had to fight to get him into a verbal classroom where he would learn from other kids and not stagnate, I had to press to get the teachers to scold him or to teach him not to imitate behaviors that were not his and not productive to his improvement.

Tyrone's physical development, weight, and height were obviously abnormal for his age. What he lacked in height and weight, he gained in intelligence. His spasticity diminished entirely as he grew older and he gained even more dexterity of his hands and improvement to his upper body motor skills. He could write, draw, and play with boy-things like his peers with some improvising. I think because he sat in a wheelchair, he spent much of his time observing things that other children didn't because they were active. Even as a younger child, he was the only kid in the family to recognize that one of his uncles wore a toupee and my mother walked with a limp. He called a broom a "sweep" because every time someone reached for the broom they said they were going to sweep the floor. His perception made sense; we don't "broom" the floor. He imagined and formulated ideas from a wheelchair and not from physical exploration and interaction with others like regular kids did.

We take for granted the importance of the smell of a flower, the touch of a furry animal, and the cool ocean water brushing our feet, but a child in a wheelchair yearns to do those seemingly small things on his own. All his life Tyrone had to be with Jacky and me and was limited in his choices because our life was his life and not one of his own. He never got his face dirty, his pants ripped, or his knees scraped. I wonder how many curiosities he had but couldn't venture out on his own to explore? He was a boy without a sport and a teenager without a girlfriend. He didn't have a paper route and never traveled alone. But, he did have parents and family who expressed in their everyday demeanor that he was loved and supported.

We take for granted the importance of the smell of a flower, the touch of a furry animal, and the cool ocean water brushing our feet, but a child in a wheelchair yearns to do those seemingly small things on his own.

FRIENDS, FAMILY, AND FUN TIMES

Don't get me wrong; Tyrone may have been limited in his choices, but he didn't lack enjoyment in life. He had a sense of adventure that you couldn't help but smile at. Boonie, Raina's son and my nephew, loved taking Tyrone with him. Boonie, despite his silly nickname, was a 6'1" handsome hunk of a young man. At the age of twenty-three, he was a suave ladies' man. Boonie had wavy dark brown hair, tan skin, and muscles that protruded through his shirt. He had small eyes and lips that slanted upward into a slight show of his teeth, giving him a gorgeous smile. He wanted to teach Tyrone street smarts. Tyrone tried to take on Boonie's persona whenever he was with him, displaying the same charm and blush on his face as if he was a ladies' man too. Tyrone was quite the suave dresser himself. As mentioned before, like Jacky and me, he loved clothes. He loved to dress up, always looking like a true gentleman and charming those around him. Every morning at school, the teachers gathered at the school's front door watching to see what Tyrone was wearing when he got off the bus. Like Boonie, he had the charisma and charm to woo them. In fact, he did it to me on a daily basis. Growing up, one of the cutest things Tyrone used to do to me was kiss my cheek if I happened to lean my face by his face. If I sat next to him on the couch, he would touch my hand. He was always affectionate, and he wanted his dad to be more affectionate toward me, too. Jacky was laid-back, shy, and quiet, not much of a public Casanova personality like Tyrone or Boonie. Tyrone would say admirable things about me to challenge his dad, like "Isn't ma the best cook?" or "Doesn't ma look nice in that dress?" Jacky seldom took the bait. I guess he caught on to Tyrone's schemes and, like me, appreciated this sweet, observant side of our son.

Growing up, one of the cutest things Tyrone used to do to me was kiss my cheek if I happened to lean my face by his face.

Boonie worked at a dingy bar in the Strip District—a working class neighborhood down by the old fruit markets, railroad, and Eastern European markets—and I think he snuck Tyrone into the bar a few times. There is no telling what else they did. Ty—as they called him—would never tell, but the guilty look on his face said everything. One

FRIENDS, FAMILY, AND FUN TIMES

time I had to rescue Tyrone and Boonie from downtown. They were supposed to be at the Pittsburgh Arts Festival. Boonie parked his car in a tow-away zone, and of course his car was towed to the city impound lot. While I worried when Tyrone was out and about in the world with his buddies, this is the kind of thing he loved: adventure. He lived his life—the one he desired—through Boonie and others for sure. I always looked at both Ty and Boonie out of the side of my eyes because I knew their adventure that day was a secret among "us guys." It was one of those "whatever happens with Boonie, stays with Boonie" kinds of things.

Growing up, Sonja and Tyrone had a great relationship too. They were typical siblings and buddies. When they were young kids, Sonja never really resented Tyrone; she just treated him like most sisters who did not always want to babysit their younger siblings. She may have envied the attention that was poured over him from everyone that got to know him, but as a little girl she didn't show it. Most people are drawn to people with outward and interesting personalities, and no doubt, Tyrone was unique in that way. Sonja often went to the movies with her little brother and her date. She didn't mind having him around and neither did her date. He was often the background observer when she interacted with and entertained her friends. Tyrone was such an intricate part of our family that even boyfriends looked forward to spending time with him as well as Sonja. I think my husband and I set the standard for making Tyrone's handicap transparent. You never really noticed it because he was so much more than the two wheels he rode around in. The fact that he was always around made you look for him to be always around.

It was a rare occasion to see my husband and I without Tyrone or vice versa. We called ourselves "The Three Amigos." We tried to treat Tyrone like a normal kid without the thought of his illness in the back of our minds. Jacky took Tyrone to high school football games, and we went on vacation to other cities—including trips to Atlanta to visit my husband's family—exposing him to the world around him. Once, on a trip to Florida while we visited Walt Disney World and a cousin, we wheeled Tyrone into the Atlantic Ocean so that he could feel the cool water on his feet. It was a wonderful experience for him, but not a good thing for a steel-trimmed wheelchair. The wet salty water on the wheelchair wheels rusted and corroded the spokes after they dried. But it was no biggie—it was worth it. When the worst has already happened in your life, everything else seems minuscule.

Tyrone loved Walt Disney World. I think it was a special trip given to Tyrone by my mother; she often singled out

FRIENDS, FAMILY, AND FUN TIMES

ones in the family that were disadvantaged and treated them to special things. So on occasion, my mother would do something special for him because he didn't have the freedom and opportunities like her other grandchildren. Sonja wasn't on the trip, and even as a grown woman, she still feels rejection about that day. I think she probably had to go to school and stay with relatives that day. I know it wasn't intentional, but it was not sensitive enough on our part, which happened on occasion as we worried incessantly about Tyrone and trying to expose him to the things other kids naturally enjoyed.

We were protective of Tyrone, but we still always loved our daughter. Like a typical sibling rivalry, Sonja did eventually and naturally become resentful of the attention Tyrone was getting. While she was previously just happy to be included and relished his little improvements like the rest of us did, at some point I believe certain things like the Disney trip started making her feel isolated from the rest of her family. I was too submerged in Tyrone's day-to-day challenges to notice. On occasion, I detected anger directed toward him, but I thought it was a brother/sister thing. It wasn't until she was a grown woman that I realized where all her anger most likely came from. I tried to be conscious of Tyrone's life, and in doing so, I came to understand that I overwhelmed her life, forgetting that she, too, needed extra attention now and then. I wanted her to be free and not oppressed by him. I was so worried that something would happen to Jacky and me, which would cause Sonja to be responsible for Tyrone. That was my worst nightmare. Maybe she perceived this differently. Maybe I should have tried harder. Regardless, my intentions were good, but her feelings were still hurt. This was something that we would spend many years resolving.

Of course, other family members also paid Tyrone special attention. Gran, Jacky's grandmother, came to live with us for a little while until we were able to find her a place to live with a nice caregiver. She was a sweet soul and she loved her grandchildren and great grandchildren. One Christmas morning, at the sound of a firetruck's siren, she jumped out of bed and ran out the front door into the freezing cold with just her nightgown on to flag Santa Claus down as he rode up our street. "Santa" did this every year. He sat in a big firetruck tossing candy out to the kids while the sirens screeched loudly, signaling them to come outside. Gran wasn't going to let Santa pass up her great grandson. She ran into the street, stood directly in front of the firetruck waving her arms, and cried out for Santa to please come give her crippled great grandson some candy too. Santa was happy to come into the house

FRIENDS, FAMILY, AND FUN TIMES

to personally give Tyrone candy, and Tyrone was so happy to see Santa.

Shortly after Gran moved, Sonja became pregnant in her senior year of high school. Our home—or maybe I should say our lives—was never lacking challenges and uninvited excitement. Sonja continued going to school, participating in events, accepting awards, and receiving her diploma with the pride of her peers as if nothing had changed. When she gave birth to Monica, she even insisted on a natural delivery and breastfeeding her little girl. Tyrone was very happy when Monica was born. He felt like an adult man because he had the grown-up title of Uncle Ty. He enjoyed holding her, and when she was old enough, he talked to her like he was the surrogate father. After Monica was a year old, Sonja attended the University of Pittsburgh to get her bachelor's degree. She was home most evenings being a mother. When she wasn't home, I was the doting grandmother filling in for the mother. Sonja never shrugged her responsibilities or obligations to Monica, as well as her commitment to finish college and follow her dreams. She was student by day and mommy by evening, and she excelled in both. We all pitched in to support her; helping with little Monica was a pleasure for all of us—Tyrone, Jacky, and I. She was the healthy bundle of joy Jacky and I hoped for.

GRAIN OF HOPE

Yet again, it was time to move; we needed more space. After being in our ranch-style house for nine years, we moved to a historical neighborhood full of large Victorian-style homes. We chose the house we moved into because the architect that lived there redesigned the house to make it accessible for his daughter who also was in a wheelchair. It was a very stately home with high ceilings, stained glass windows, and a grand stained glass front door with stained glass skylights. It had so many wonderful features we just loved. There was a wonderful wood-burning fireplace, a foyer that included a piano, and an elevator that went from the basement to the second floor. The house had a very long wood-railed porch that Tyrone enjoyed sitting on as he watched the neighbors walk by. Even the lawn was perfect, with a nice oriental-style landscape that hid a wheelchair ramp. The house had everything. Needless to say, we had plenty of room and space for the wheelchair, a little girl, and an active family of five to move around freely.

Tyrone attended the same school until he graduated at the age of twenty. He even took three cousins to the prom. Yes, indeed, Mr. Popularity went to three different proms, handsomely attired, wearing an expression on his face like the cat that ate the canary. After graduation, to give Tyrone opportunities to be in a "normal" environment, I enrolled

FRIENDS, FAMILY, AND FUN TIMES

him in an algebra course at the community college. It was a non-credit course for young kids. The only downfall was that we had to ride up to his classroom on the second floor in a stinky freight elevator located near the garbage court. It was the only elevator in the building. But, it was well worth it to see the proud look on Tyrone's face as he solved problems and got more correct answers than other children; he did exceptionally well. His interacting with other students, talking on their level, and watching their expressions of admiration for him was priceless. After all the years of struggle, he triumphed. It was important for him to believe that, just because he was different, didn't mean he was not equal to others his age. Activities like this were great confidence builders too.

Yes, indeed, Mr. Popularity went to three different proms, handsomely attired, wearing an expression on his face like the cat that ate the canary.

A SHATTERED DREAM

We actually thought that death had forgotten about Tyrone. We had been so busy living, trying to enjoy a "normal" life and enjoying our time with him. Sorry to say, eventually death remembered him. For twenty years, he bravely prevailed over one obstacle after another. But scoliosis and deteriorating cartilage in his rib cage were the beginning of the end of a hard-fought battle to survive Conradi-Hunermann syndrome. It became obvious that he had ascended to the peak of his life, and at the ripe old age of twenty it was clear he had started his descent. Our entire life with Tyrone was a battle, and we were always in fighting mode. It is amazing what becomes natural. We were brave soldiers with calluses on our backs from battle. We won many battles, but we were losing the war.

It was clear Tyrone was deteriorating. He had regular doctor's appointments and we saw that the curve in his spine was steadily increasing; we knew it wasn't good, but there was no way to prevent it from happening. Vague signs and symptoms that were similar to Glenn's hovered over Tyrone's body, gradually robbing him of weight, muscle mass, and strength. Doctor's had to treat Tyrone's symptoms as they appeared, hopeful that they could overcome all of the obstacles of the debilitating disease, including deteriorating cartilage and abnormal bone growth. The disease was a mystery and so was Tyrone's ability to live with it. He had responded to therapy and other surgeries well previously, so why not now? After all, Tyrone had proven them wrong before and lived much longer than the predicted six months.

> *The disease was a mystery and so was Tyrone's ability to live with it.*

Gradually, Tyrone's spine continued to curve to the point that he leaned uncomfortably to one side as his back began to bow. We thought we had escaped the worst, but time proved we didn't. Something had to be done—another serious decision had to be made. Again, there were the ebbs and flows in our lives. Tyrone carefully listened as the orthopedic doctor explained the degree of the curve in his back. Physically, anyone could see it was extreme. The doctor told us that if it continued to curve, and it would, he was sure to be paralyzed. The prognosis was not delivered in a caring way. I felt that the delivery was clinical, cold, and quite direct. I didn't feel like I could ask any questions. I took the doctor's words as gospel, as I always had, and accepted it. Over the years, most of the doctors were more focused on the procedures at hand, and I tried to get used to what I perceived as arrogance and condescension and chalked it all up to poor bedside manner. But it was hard; it had always been hard. My little guy, not used to this type of demeanor or language, was very frightened by the thought of being "paralyzed." His eyes widened, and he shook his head no, no, no. He didn't want to be paralyzed. And of course, he was not alone. We were all saddened and let down. Even though it sickened us, our hearts went out to Tyrone. We didn't exhibit selfish emotions or thoughts; all sorrow was for him. Though I fought to keep my cool, we were somber and did not overreact. We gathered our thoughts, walked away, and went on with our lives with another dark cloud dangling over our heads. Experience taught us to be patient and not to panic.

The options included the possibility of becoming paralyzed from the surgery or positively becoming paralyzed without it. Tyrone wanted to make the decision. He was mature enough and we let him. We thought it would be easier for him to accept any outcome of his own decision rather than ours, especially if the operation didn't turn out for the best. We didn't want to risk him being angry with us or feeling like he had no control over his own destiny and life.

Anxiety and fear were back in our lives again after we had been doing so well without them. I understood Tyrone's choice to undergo surgery. He was a smart kid and knew enough to understand that he only had one choice left to make. Scoliosis made the choice for him; he just had to verbalize it. The effects of the disease had caught up to him. His curved spine and the deterioration of cartilage that made his rib cage begin to cave in made bodily processes we don't even think about—like breathing and digestion—increasingly difficult. Severe cases of scoliosis prevent the heart, lungs, and stomach from expanding, leading to extreme discomfort and failure to thrive. I can't say I knew this day would come, because I sincerely thought it wouldn't. I thought this was just another challenge and another chance to meet a crisis head-on. We had become so courageous as a family. We never told him Conradi-Hunermann syndrome was fatal; therefore, he wasn't expecting to get worse. Tyrone maintained a positive attitude because he was a proven warrior. All that was left to do was what we had always done: pray for him, love him, and support him. Prayers, love, and support had brought him this far. We were fortified in faith; I had struggled and questioned God before, but years of loving my sweet boy Tyrone and living such a positive life with him brought me back to God's side in my rightful place.

After the surgery, with disappointment in his voice, the doctor informed us the surgery did not go as planned. It was too difficult to get the correction he needed and was trying to achieve. Poor Sonja, she was so disappointed, she cried. She knew how much the success of the surgery meant to her little brother and the thought of being paralyzed was paralyzing in itself. It was a baffling disappointment. We were so sure everything would be fine. That was a very sad and somber day. All of the air was out of our sails and the tears flowed. We couldn't wrap our minds around what this meant at the time.

She knew how much the success of the surgery meant to her little brother and the thought of being paralyzed was paralyzing in itself.

We didn't let Tyrone know the surgery was not a success. What real purpose would it serve? It would probably make him give up on life and we wanted him to live whatever life he had left to the fullest. There he lied in a hospital bed with a full body cast from chest to hip and all for what? After a short stay in the hospital, we brought him home—cast and all—to recuperate. He was given a welcome home party and the family cheered him on like a superstar. Most of the time, we tried to have family events and holidays celebrated at our house anyway because it was more convenient and less exhausting with his wheelchair and braces. Tyrone loved his family. He had many cousins, aunts, uncles, and friends, and they were exceptional at returning their love for him. He was always the center of attention, and it was easy to see that he fancied himself in the spotlight—such a character. That night, they showered him with love and well wishes. Our family has and always remains a supportive bunch of great folks. Even to this day, we love to get together for birthdays, holidays, and just for the heck of it.

But as if bad news from the surgeon was not enough, Tyrone started hemorrhaging shortly after coming home. He was rushed to the emergency room where they frantically pumped blood plasma into his veins to keep him alive. As fast as the blood plasma went in was as fast as his blood came out. The bleeding kept coming and coming; they couldn't stop it. It was decided to do an emergency surgery to find the problem and stop the bleeding. We waited in the hospital's chapel where we could pray. That night, Tyrone escaped the hands of death for the second time. During the whole hurly-burly, he acted like a real sport, even apologizing for inconveniencing the doctors and nurses. It was the middle of the night and he had enough experience with doctors and hospitals to know that they were called away from their personal lives on account of him. Who apologizes like that? Only a caring, unselfish person would do that.

An artery break caused the hemorrhaging. It was able to be repaired but he remained in critical condition in the ICU. I slept overnight in the dark, somewhat unnerving waiting area that was not much more than an old worn leather couch at the end of a long, empty hallway. After visiting hours, the only light was the nurse's station at the other end of the hall. During the night, I would tip-toe into the ICU area where Tyrone lie almost lifeless in the bed to let him know I was there. I would speak softly in his ear and tightly hold his hand. He had a breathing tube in his mouth and was unable to talk. His response was good readings on his monitors. On occasion, the nurse would come get me during the night when his monitor readings dipped too low or climbed too high. When I was at his bedside he always stabilized. This went on for several days and nights. There were tubes everywhere, and I'm sure listening to the sucking and hissing sounds of a respirator all day and night was frightening. Thankfully, Tyrone seemed to be a quick healer, maybe because he had such a positive outlook on life and a spirit to thrive. The monitor readings stayed stable, his tubes came out, and he was eating and talking, so there was no reason to keep him in the hospital. So wouldn't you just know, in no time at all, the young fighter was back home, smiling and happy as if nothing happened. He was still that gutsy little guy with true grit.

No one mentioned the word paralyzed in our house. But that didn't stop it from happening. It gradually crept over his body like a slow-moving shadow. It started with something as slight as frequently dropping his fork and not holding items tightly in his hand, to a gradual, general weakening of his extremities. In less than one year after surgery, his body shrunk into a crippled, curved, and sagged physique. All he could control was the functioning of his eyes, nose, mouth, and ears. His body had no ability to be of any use to him. What he feared overtook him. Yet he never complained, he never changed; somewhere inside of this worn-down body still lived the spirit of Tyrone.

His magnetic personality never crumbled under the destruction of the disease. He was trapped inside a crippled body that could no longer support his beautiful spirit. Tyrone fought back an ugly disease that paralyzed him, but he never lost hope that God would one day heal him. Trying to be positive about the future, we had just started a desktop publishing business to give Tyrone some more independence and responsibility. We continued to try giving Tyrone as much opportunity as possible to live a normal life in the face of death. Not long after we started the business, he had become a paraplegic, and after just one year in business, Tyrone was put on constant oxygen. A computer system was configured by the local children's hospital so he could continue to help with the business. The system used a straw-like device that Tyrone blew into to make keystrokes on his computer and another device that fit like a crown on his head, allowing him to browse through and select text. His body was the mouse and keypad. He could typeset text for business cards and letterhead. Most days he was weary and just out of energy, and soon he could no longer come in to work.

His magnetic personality never crumbled under the destruction of the disease. He was trapped inside a crippled body that could no longer support his beautiful spirit.

Over the next year, Tyrone's life was reminiscent of the misery and struggle for life that I had lived through twenty years ago with Glenn. Tyrone lost so much body fat that I slept with him to share my body heat. All during the night, the hiss and hum of the oxygen was heard in the dark stillness of the night. Because Tyrone's lungs weren't functioning properly, there wasn't enough oxygen in his blood, and instead there was an overabundance of carbon dioxide. Every morning I did not know if Tyrone would wake. His sleeping was getting deeper and deeper so it became increasingly difficult to arouse him from sleep. He had several "near-death sleeps." Under one of those deep sleeping spells, he claimed he saw Glenn. Tyrone thought Glen resembled himself, almost as if he were looking in the mirror. He had an out-of-body experience, I guess. The young warrior lost all his strength and his will to make it through another day. I'll never forget the night Tyrone realized his life would soon end. He turned to me that night as I laid him down for bed and affirmed, "Ma, I win if I live and I win if I die." He saw no failure in God. He knew he would live a healed life when he died and that his life had purpose here on earth and throughout eternity.

Shortly thereafter, he passed away, dying of respiratory failure. The night he died, we both had a look in our eyes of acceptance and understanding. It was crystal clear that I knew he was ready to let me go and at the same time he knew I was ready to let him go. I believe Tyrone suffered inwardly just for me for too long. Tyrone succumbed to Conradi-Hunermann syndrome, just as his brother, Glenn, had before him. He remained a shining star up until his death that cold November day. He lived to be twenty-two years old, dying peacefully in the emergency room. His journey was all over and his spirit set free.

My sons' spirits had no more capacity to reside in their emaciated bodies. They withered as dying flowers on a stem. Time stood still, and I was thoughtlessly suspended—frail, in a pitch-black space—the moment they died. However, I learned from Tyrone that, like the turning of the leaves in fall, there is great beauty in death and, as with spring, there is the hope of rebirth for the dead. Tyrone's spirit continued to impact our lives even after his death. His good friend and cousin, Boonie, who took him under his wing to make sure he could experience the world as a "normal" young man would, died at twenty-eight years old after a battle with leukemia. He stopped taking debilitating chemo medication because he had experienced enough suffering. The grace and strength with which Tyrone handled his illness and impending death surely had a profound impact on Boonie. After watching his little cousin, Boonie was able to reach a point where he was ready to let go, joining Tyrone in death. I believe Tyrone took the fear away from Boonie, and he was willing to accept death. All those years of time spent together transcended into the deaths of two childhood cousins and dear friends who impacted one another beyond the big lives they both led.

Recalling the darkest moments of death, I think accepting it in your head and not denying what you visually see is the worst. Many years of caring for Tyrone and watching the disease claim pieces of my son's body a little at a time, as any mother knows, was agonizing. Accepting that a loved one lost the battle of life is a horrific reality. Getting to that stage takes a lifetime because of a magnetic desire to refuse to say goodbye or let go. Your children are under your skin, and you can't easily shed them. They have to be forcefully snatched from you.

Part 3

A SPECIAL TYPE OF GRIEF

It was solemn on the way home after leaving the hospital where we left Tyrone's lifeless body. We felt the same lifelessness. As soon as we stepped in the house, you could sense the dark shadow of change in the atmosphere. It lost the excitement and sense of warmth that it had before. It was just Jacky and me, indescribably exhausted, saddened, and bruised. We were going to have to live in a home we purchased for a family—a family that would never live in the house with us again. It was never going to be the same. We would no longer have a need for an elevator, a wheelchair ramp, or even a wheelchair. Our lives, like our home, lost purpose and meaning in a manner of a few short hours. A battle for life fought for twenty-two years was interrupted by death in just one quick moment. We were very silent that night. The house did not have the hissing sound of the oxygen tank or the sounds of the TV Tyrone always enjoyed watching. Nothing could possibly give us pleasure there anymore. Even with the lights on, the house seemed very dark. But a beautiful thing blossomed that night, and

Jacky and I were able to openly cry in the daylight and in the presence of each other. Before that, Jacky and I were accustomed to being secretive, always hiding our emotions, not sharing our thoughts. Sometime during the evening of Tyrone's death, we undressed, quietly climbed into bed with our thoughts, and let our tears fall down our cheeks instinctively as we fell asleep together.

A battle for life fought for twenty-two years was interrupted by death in just one quick moment.

I remember feeling strange the next morning knowing that Tyrone was not in his bed. Knowing his bed was going to be empty forever was a "pinch yourself" moment. I can't remember much about the next couple days because I was in a daze. However, my body remembered its duties. We prepared for Tyrone's funeral, pulling together a burial outfit, Jacky taking as much time as he always did carefully coordinating a classy black and gray tweed sport coat, black slacks with a crisp white shirt, and a designer tie—even putting his own pinky ring on Ty's ring finger to take with him as a keepsake.

The funeral was sad, as most funerals are. There is never an easy way to say goodbye forever. We were more mature and better experienced at dealing with death than we had been with Glenn, but that's not to say it was in any way easier. We had to go on. What else could we do? At the time, we wanted to die, but we didn't. Death is out of our control. Our only choice was being alive and feeling dead. We were going through the day-to-day motions with no one home inside. I think it was more difficult for Jacky because he had to work. Or, maybe it was better for him because he could leave our lonely home and escape for a while. But after any distraction, eventually the deep, desperate feelings of reality overshadowed everything again. Somehow, without any magic potion, you get through life one day at a time. Though I know it is through the grace of a merciful God, I still wonder how we do it. How do we find a way through the pain? How did the trials that weakened us end up strengthening us and forcing us to forge forward with more appreciation for what remained of our lives?

But after any distraction, eventually the deep, desperate feelings of reality overshadowed everything again.

In the aftermath of Tyrone's death, none of us dared to say or act like we were "going crazy." It was taboo and clearly a reason to be shunned. I apologize for the politically incorrect expression, "crazy," but I just thought I would invite you into my generation. Whether you were crazy or emotionally unstable, both words got the same "stay away" reaction. Unfortunately, there were not too many shoulders to cry on and not too many willing and understanding ears to listen. You had to be tough because times required it. Everyone had some problem that they were dealing with alone, I'm sure. Thankfully, we always had each other.

When I hear people under pressure speak of a grinding wheel inside them, I truly understand what they mean. My wheel was grinding day and night and there appeared to be no end in sight. Many times I was irritated, and unfortunately I took it out on anyone and everyone that I felt hassled me or criticized my behavior. Sonja and Jacky bore the brunt of my wrath throughout the years since Glenn had passed—Jacky because it seemed he was never there to help, burying himself at the plant, and Sonja because she was always there needing my care and time when I was already overwhelmed. The guilt Jacky and I both shared feeling everything was our fault took many years to overcome, if we ever did. Yet, we managed to keep picking up the pieces in our lives and pushing forward under extreme conditions. When I reflect back, I realize that I had an unbelievably cohesive family. Life is

A SPECIAL TYPE OF GRIEF

similar to a beautiful rose; it has great beauty, but there are thorns. I believe the thorny trials and tribulations in my family created a deep and enduring love for each other. We were ordained to stay together forever because we had already come through an out-of-this-world experience. Life in crisis taught us to lock arms together and endure to the finish, moving onward and trusting God no matter what.

Life is similar to a beautiful rose; it has great beauty, but there are thorns.

A BEAUTIFUL TRIBUTE

(Read at Tyrone's funeral)

A beautiful unquenchable spirit trapped in a broken body. Christ was broken in body and set free. He had no opportunity for sin; thus, he was Christ-like.

Tyrone was an inspiration to all of us. He was cheerful, loving, giving, concerned.

A tribute goes to his parents and sister whose years of love kept him sustained.

His leaving was untimely in our minds, but... he fulfilled his goals within his lifespan. Tyrone accomplished more than most of us do in a much longer lifetime.

Because of God's gifts to Tyrone he was able to minister to us. His maturity, intelligence, and loving spirit taught all of us lessons we should always remember.

Let us celebrate his life.

—Barbara McCollum Hart, Cousin

LIFE, DEATH, AND FINDING AN ACCEPTABLE PEACE

At a very young age, I was faced with the raw realities of life and death. I had no reason to think about death, and therefore when death happened I really couldn't wrap my mind around it. Even after many years have gone by, I still ponder death's piercing effects on me and the ongoing challenge to manage its lingering, permanent, hurtful emotions. Back then I was young, full of hope for a bright future with my husband, and looking forward to having several children. We were healthy, and we were excited about all the possibilities we had as a young husband and wife. But life had a different plan for us, one I would never have expected. Who would have ever thought death would claim the fragile lives of not just one, but four of our children?

These precious babies lived and grew inside my body. All of nature's wonderful emotions culminated into praises of love the day they were born. No other person has ever been or will ever be as endearing to a parent's affections as one's own child. My children were part of my body; they shared my spirit as I shared theirs. The anticipation of life and the preparation in my heart and mind were indelible. Bringing a new life into the world was a sweet and everlasting gift from me to my husband and in turn, his sweet and everlasting gift to me. Our children's births were to be a time of happiness and readiness, looking forward to the bright future of a loving young family. All of my children—Sonja, Glenn, Tyrone, Patrick, and baby boy Williams—were formed in love embodying two people into one. And yet, four of them were stolen by death.

> *My children were part of my body; they shared my spirit as I shared theirs.*

Every conscientious parent nurtures and loves their young unconditionally. Parents look upon their children as their future, their personal contribution to society, and the continuation of their seed or family tree. In a normal situation, children are protected (and sometimes overprotected) by parents standing guard over their lives. We love everything about them from their sweet new baby smell to their independent spirits as they grow in front of our eyes. Often, parents are so blinded and deafened by love that they deny any negative truths about their

LIFE, DEATH, AND FINDING AN ACCEPTABLE PEACE

children. My sons were extremely disabled from the day they were born, and I was in so much denial over it because I was blinded by my love for them. I didn't see their imperfections; I only saw my precious little boys. Love is life's strongest emotion, but it does blind us to so many things.

I knew what was happening over the course of time, and when I look back, I can clearly see what fate was going to bring all of us. That doesn't change the pain I felt nor does it change the emptiness I still feel when I look back on those days. When your child dies, death creates a permanent hole in your heart. I think there is a spiritual reason: a piece of your soul goes with them. I sincerely believe it takes God to fill the emptiness. Once this hole is patched with God's love, you grow and flourish into a witness for others with the strength to impart hope in others who are hurting or suffering in silence. God's love did it for me.

Children are your flesh and blood. They are loved, they are innocent, and you want so much to protect them. We want to believe that bad things don't happen to babies and children, that they don't die and that innocent people don't have to endure such pain.

But they do. We do. I did.

I often compare the pain of losing a child to losing a limb. People who have lost limbs often report that they still feel their missing limbs. Is this because the brain remembers and the soul is resistant to the change? Even if you get a high-tech prosthetic, it will never function like your own limb. You can learn to use the prosthetic, but it will never feel like your real limb. Even if it works, it may be an acceptable fact of life, but it will never be the same. Your soul yearns for a sense of peace—a sense of how life once was or was supposed to be.

I often compare the pain of losing a child to losing a limb. People who have lost limbs often report that they still feel their missing limbs.

SONJA: A REFLECTION ON MY DAUGHTER

I say that my family was cohesive and we stuck together, but maybe that was just what we presented to the outside world. On the inside, there was anger, pain, and envy. This was evident in Sonja more than anyone, though it didn't come to light until Tyrone passed. For more years than I care to give a number, my daughter built an angry wall between us. She may not be aware of it, but it has fallen on me several times. That is not to say I always understood why, because for many years I didn't. I didn't see the whole picture until I reflected on the past using Sonja's childhood eyes and not mine. Struggling to save our sons shoved away our daughter. After Tyrone passed, I was confronted with that realization head on. When Sonja was young, we were not mature enough to know that our crisis was disrupting a family's delicate balance. We had only been a family a short time, so for us, the bar was still being set; we were new to everything. We weren't well-versed in parenthood, let alone illnesses and critical medical issues.

Struggling to save our sons shoved away our daughter.

Do the present and future resolve the regrets of the past? I am hopeful that they do. Until then, the present is a perfect time for reflection, understanding, and healing. During tragedy, there is always a whole picture to look at, not one single focal point. If I can reach just one person, please try to understand my message. Without awareness, a problem or crisis can be so doggone consuming that it is capable of victimizing innocent family members and friends. The consuming drive to spend an inordinate amount of time dealing with tragedy is very normal. But be careful, because most often the flip side of one problem may cause you to create another. In our case, we tried so hard to balance our boys and their issues with a "normal" family life. At the same time, we thought we were protecting our daughter by leaving her with others so that she could play or have fun and not experience the daily pain of it all. Instead, we ended up never truly seeing her—her face, her needs, and her love for us.

SONJA: A REFLECTION ON MY DAUGHTER

I'll never forget the time when Sonja was eight years old and taking violin lessons; that day will stick with me the rest of my life. We never tried to neglect Sonja. Of course, we loved her just as much as we loved Tyrone. But, in giving him the best care we could muster, Sonja was sometimes left by the wayside. It wasn't just the big Disney World trip, but the day-to-day activities that affected her most. One day, I didn't have a way to pick her up after violin lessons because I didn't have any transportation that day and there wasn't anyone to watch Tyrone. So, I took a chance. I gave her a very detailed explanation and a note about how to catch the bus and where to get off. This was going to be her first trip alone. I thought she was old enough for this venture; it was a safe world back then and the bus stops were just across from where her lessons took place and just around the corner from our house. However, the bus she caught was on its last run and was not going to the stop where she was told to get off around the corner from our house.

You can't imagine the panic that gripped me when Sonja didn't show up on time that afternoon. I couldn't go looking for her because I couldn't leave Tyrone. I didn't want to leave a defenseless child in the house alone, but it was going to be dark soon and I couldn't leave Sonja out there by herself to get lost or taken. I called the police

GRAIN OF HOPE

and then Jacky at work. Jacky was not the type to worry outwardly unless really necessary, and the police said I had to wait 24 hours to report a missing person. All I could think was, Sonja isn't a person yet! She's just a little girl! To say I was frightened to death and at my wits end would be putting it mildly. Hearing the desperation in my voice, one officer sympathized with me and came to the house anyway. He filled out a report and assured me he would do what he could to help find Sonja.

Just as dusk was approaching, over the horizon appeared a welcoming sight. Little Sonja, walking slowly, had finally come home. The terrifying thoughts going through my mind came to an abrupt stop. All I could feel was happy. She walked all the way from a bus stop that was about 3 miles away—quite a distance to walk up and down steep hills for a young, fragile girl. I'm glad Sonja had the wherewithal to avoid getting into someone's car or going to a stranger's house. Thank God she wasn't harmed in any way, but she was pretty exhausted and a bit frightened after walking alone for such a long distance. She was glad to be home so she could finally get some rest. Sonja was always good at figuring things out, probably because she had learned to be an only child despite having siblings. For me, that was the longest day of my life. But the blessing is, it ended well.

SONJA: A REFLECTION ON MY DAUGHTER

As my relief over having Sonja back was replaced with exhaustion, I became immensely angry with the bus driver for not being more conscientious and not notifying the authorities that a little girl was stranded. I learned a valuable lesson that day. I cared about her so much, and it was time I started showing it more. That was the first and last time I let Sonja catch a bus or go anywhere alone again until she was much, much older.

We learn significant lessons from the past, and then we use that knowledge as a basis for making decisions in the present and the future. During an upheaval, odds are that a loved one who you think can endure is the one who may be more vulnerable. My boys were so fragile and sick, and my daughter was able-bodied and curious. I never thought that Sonja could be the vulnerable one because she didn't share the same disease as her brothers; I had neglected to see the emotional vulnerability she was hiding. As parents, we were the comfort and the stability she needed and she just wanted to know that she mattered too. Too often, these revelations arrive late. Keeping a family together during a crisis requires strength most of us do not possess. Statistics reveal that families typically fall apart during bad times. I guess you could say our family's strong bond of love and tenacity was our "crazy glue," but that's not to say we had no broken seals.

GRAIN OF HOPE

We learn significant lessons from the past, and then we use that knowledge as a basis for making decisions in the present and the future.

In the aftermath of Tyrone's death, Sonja and I went through a rough patch. I had finally been confronted with how much we had unintentionally neglected her. We limped along as mother and daughter, distant in each other's lives. We were robbed of the closeness and intimacy mothers and daughters traditionally share. I shielded smart remarks and angry looks, likely intended to reveal any lingering resentment.

Still, we didn't turn our backs on each other, and we appreciated the relationship we did have. I always felt left out of her fun yet honored to be brought into her concerns whenever she needed advice or guidance. Without the warm and cozy feelings for each other, we continued our roles as mother and daughter and in time, emotions gradually healed because of a persistence to be part of each other's life. I think it took maturity on Sonja's part to understand the many complicated facets of our family. I believe she learned through the word of God that a person's anger and anxiety only diminish you. And by nature, Sonja is a caring and giving person. Jacky always assured me that

SONJA: A REFLECTION ON MY DAUGHTER

her heart and mine would soften. I guess he knew us better than we did.

It is a miracle that Sonja is a grounded and confident young woman. She was a young mother like I was. That never prevented her from enriching herself with education, marriage, a business, and a career. She attains goals that she sets for herself and has the courage to meet any challenge. I wonder where she gets the strength that she has to tackle such things on her own. Any parent would be proud to call her daughter. My soul is calm because the outcome is that Sonja is happy. She is my role model, the cornerstone and foundation of my life. I love and admire the woman she has become. She is a wonderful legacy my husband and I gave to the world. Today, Sonja and I happily live within a few miles of each other, functioning together without the previous animosity. There is no need to rehash years gone by and no need for more apologies. We enjoy each other and I am so happy that she continues to celebrate our family traditions. Life happened and we are okay. All is forgiven.

MOVING ON: JACKY AND ME

When people get married, they always say you either sink or swim. It seemed our whole married life had been swimming upstream against rough tide, but somehow we kept on swimming. Our friends had always thought Jacky and I were a "cute couple." I was the yin to his yang for sure. We were two very willing hearts eager to explore this thing called love and marriage and family. However, we hadn't been much of a couple for our whole married lives. We knew each other as parents—as caretakers—not necessarily as lovers or a more traditional married couple; the intimate knowing of one another was gone the moment Conradi-Hunermann syndrome took over our lives. In the privacy of our home, I called Jacky "brother man" and he called me "sister woman." At times, it seemed we were more like siblings. Tyrone called us "dad boy" and "mommy girl." We were kids when we married and I think in some ways we stayed kids to our kids.

Still, when Jacky and I had a chance to spend time together, we enjoyed it. Our quiet time together consisted of watching Turner Classic Movies, interesting documentaries, The History Channel, and National Geographic programming. We were not your typical soap opera or Action Jackson people. I guess you could say that real life and the more serious side of life appealed to us more. We did love comedy though. We had fun joking around with each other and laughing together during a good Jerry Lewis or Rodney Dangerfield skit. I would characterize us as a comedy team like Ricky and Lucy Ricardo from the 1950's TV series I Love Lucy. We also enjoyed the nightlife and bright lights. Back in the 80's, Jacky and I frequented many of the musical venues and stage shows in our beloved city of Pittsburgh. Jacky was a jazz buff and we visited most of the jazz scenes in the city. We seldom missed concerts at the Manchester Craftsmen's Guild or the annual Pitt jazz concert. I wanted to travel, which was almost impossible until we had an empty nest and money to purchase a timeshare vacation plan. The combination of enjoying our fine city and traveling was the perfect mix for our enjoyment.

When we became empty-nesters after Tyrone's passing, you could say we started to catch up on life. We were imprisoned by Conradi-Hunermann syndrome and the effects it had on our boys; we couldn't develop like a normal couple. After all, we were still kids ourselves when we got married and began having kids. As time went on, we only knew one another as parents. Knowing each other as individuals quickly faded away because it was all about our kids and very little about us. When we were taking care of the boys and Sonja, we couldn't plan anything. We had to take the time to do things together when we had the chance, which was few and far between. Naturally, after Tyrone passed, we didn't really know what to do with ourselves. We felt like we were starting all over again, and so after twenty years of being married, we were restarting the process. Getting to know one another twenty years into the marriage wasn't something we imagined, but Jacky and I had come to expect the unexpected. Together, Jacky and I ran free. We ran until we were exhausted, taking in all the joys of life that we missed all those years. Black and white movies, jazz music, shopping in other cities, visiting upscale restaurants—suddenly we had a greater appreciation for all of the things we had always loved but failed to truly experience. We hosted cookouts and parties and everyone considered us socialites because of it—the two young grandparents we were. We wanted to do everything before we died because we realized that life was fragile and death could happen at any time.

We continued to actively enjoy life as best we could. We moved into a house near where Sonja lived for just the two of us, and enjoyed gardening and growing flowers at our new home. For a short time, I continued to operate the business we originally started to give Tyrone independence. It was nice to have our individual freedom. If Jacky wanted to do something without me, it was okay. And likewise if I wanted to do something without him. We traveled at least twice a year to islands and popular cities in the United States. We could make plans that were not interrupted. We could stay away from home without being concerned about issues at home. I must say, feeling relaxed and free from worry was wonderful.

I realize all of this sounds as if life went on without a blip. I wish I could say our lives together jump-started smoothly and problem free after Tyrone's death. But they didn't. Not only did bridge-building have to be performed to reach Sonja, there were cracks in our marriage foundation that started to widen and become much harder to fill. As with most deaths, there is enough anger, guilt, blame, and shame to go around. These emotions are common after you thaw out and reality sets in—sort of the aftershock. However, when it occurs it is surreal and most damning. It is amazing how two people that fortified each other in a crisis fell apart after the battle. I've made it seem like all was easy—the understanding family, strong show of strength by parents, and what have you. But it wasn't. Jacky and I still went through anger and guilt that constantly threatened our relationship after Tyrone died. It wasn't spoken, but you could see it in other ways. Someone always needs to be blamed. Who was at fault? Was it Jacky's fault my sons were handicapped or was it my body not being adequate enough to bear normal children? There were secret feelings and unspoken questions, but they were real questions that we constantly wondered about and tried to figure out. You just want to know why. Someone always feels angry and irritable at the other person or even themselves. My beautiful union with Jacky fractured and split into an awful separation of two soulmates that at one time fit together perfectly.

These emotions are common after you thaw out and reality sets in—sort of the aftershock.

A crisis is such a life-shattering occurrence. Nerves are raw, and you are at your wits end. After all the numbness and the shock melts away, left standing are two broken bodies that need mending and two weary souls needing help. Left to ourselves, we began to spew contemptible accusations toward each other. It was nothing in particular—everything was wrong. In the chaos of it all, I didn't realize it was the by-product of all the painful feelings that we had feverishly suppressed for too many years. The couple that once supported each other was constantly disagreeing with each other, literally picking each other apart with hurtful words and inconsiderate, petty accusations. From your skirt is too short to your tie is ugly, things that were never important became a point to argue about. We went through periods of disdain for each other over money and family decisions. The things we loved about each other were not enough anymore to keep us friends. Like any relationship, there were periods that we strayed from each other. At one point, Jacky even moved out, leaving me to fend for myself. I wish I could say he only left once, but one time he left for one week and another time for a month. Once, he was even gone for eighteen months. Unlike the previous two times before, this time I didn't know where he moved to and we had no communication. I'm sure Sonja knew and I can assure you that he kept in touch with her. I didn't interfere because I knew she was in a difficult spot trying to be loyal to both parents. I thought he surely wasn't coming back. Yet, he somehow always came home; I had even helped him pack up his things to come back once. Each time after he came back, he was extremely remorseful.

I am so thankful for my undying faith in God and the wisdom He gave me because with it, I was able to make due and maintain a positive perspective during difficult times. Here Jacky and I were, twenty years since Tyrone's death, still punishing each other. After all we endured together, I was not going to let my love and respect for my husband die too. I didn't want to let this small portion of pain Jacky and I were creating for each other cancel out over forty years of marriage. Isn't it amazing how we suffered together all those years—burying four of our children—and kept it together, yet we could not do the same for each other? We were in a battle for our own lives.

In the end, it all turned out and we became a healthy family, inclusive of our daughter and grandchildren. I guess I knew deep in my heart and Jacky knew deep in his that we were always going to have a special love and respect for one other. We were made for each other. I always attributed the problems we experienced to the aftershock of all that had happened in our lives. Our emotions that were not dealt with did not go away, and all that we suppressed had to float to the top sooner or later. We were not the same people anymore. We were older and that distance apart ultimately gave us time to think and reflect on our lives without each other. You could say reuniting was us embracing our differences and frailties and believing we were better off staying together because we were part of each other. I guess it was obvious life was not going to be fair toward us and we accepted that. We went about living with what we had left and appreciated and accepted each other. Our relationship never had the chance to grow into a sweep you off your feet romance; it was more of an understanding love and enjoyment and respect for each other type of romance. And, we were happy with that. It was a rocky road to normalcy and I am glad to say we bumped along until we made it.

> *I guess it was obvious life was not going to be fair toward us and we accepted that.*

However, three years into our newfound utopia, it came crashing to a halt when Jacky was diagnosed with amyloidosis, a rare disease that causes calcium deposits to form in the bone marrow and spread throughout the body, threatening the normal functions of organs in its path. It all started with a swollen leg and foot. Edema is a major symptom and fatal factor of the disease, and if you don't have organ failure, you will surely drown in your own body fluids. The ten months that followed after his diagnosis were very touch and go. Jacky actually had a stem cell transplant to try to combat the disease, but amyloidosis is quite resistant to any treatment. I watched my handsome husband and the father of my children wither into a very

MOVING ON: JACKY AND ME

sick and worn-out man. On December 10, 2009 and at the age of sixty-three, Jacky took his last breath sitting in the front passenger seat of Sonja's car. They were on their way to our granddaughter's basketball game.

Some things in life are just so difficult they are impossible to fully accept. Negative thoughts can disturb your peace day and night. It seems so unfair that your life is altered and you spend most of each day trying to adjust or twist things around in your mind, struggling to make even the slightest sense of what happened so that you can get through the day. It's like driving a car with an annoying engine noise. You can muzzle the sound sometimes with distractions like music and conversation, but at the end of the day in the silence and stillness of the night, the noise can still be heard. Attempting to quiet the noise feels never-ending. Yet one day after many years of exercising hope and faith, it becomes an easier burden to carry, a softer noise to silence. I believe it is easier because carrying the heavy load long enough builds the muscles that it takes to make the load seem lighter. The load weighs the same, but hope and faith have increased your strength. The situation stayed the same, but you changed. This is the essence of acceptable peace. This is what God and a little hope will do.

GRAIN OF HOPE

 I consider myself an expert in overcoming grief because of my experience with my sons and Jacky's death. Death isn't easy; it just has to be accepted. Acceptance goes a long way when you resolve in your heart it's your only choice. Sometimes the answer is so simple. After all the many years of dealing with pain and suffering, the sting was taken away through the power of loving God first in all circumstances. This relay of love between God and me lightens the challenges of all that I went through and I am assured that it will always perform the same way in the future. Take it from someone who knows; it is the only defense that wins in the end. Believing that there is a God who sincerely loves me and me sincerely loving Him in return is more than sufficient.

ACTIVATING THE POWER OF HOPE

We are guided by our feelings. Feelings determine our decisions and the paths we take in life for either the good or bad. Hope has the overwhelming power to change your life or the way you feel. Faith, on the other hand, is connected to a religion or a higher being, a dependence on supernatural help. In my religion, faith believes that there is a loving God standing by your side to help and direct your steps. He is not a feeling or imagination; He is a spiritual overseer of your life. He is the right path—all truth and enlightenment. And most importantly, He promises eternal life with Him after death. You must believe and trust He will make everything all right. I didn't start my life out with faith of my own. Like most people, I inherited my religion because my parents raised me that way. Yet, beyond the religious upbringing, I personally realized His power in my life. A crisis put me on a path to hope and hope was the bridge to faith in God. I believe very strongly that there is a power greater than fragile little me. I talk to this power; I believe and depend on this power. This power is God.

A crisis put me on a path to hope and hope was the bridge to faith in God.

Hope led me to discover my own faith, and ultimately, an intimacy with God, the giver of the power. Pain is just one pathway to God; there are others. Prayer was a vital part of my day. It's amazing how the emotional pain and desperation caused me to reach out to God, miraculously becoming the source God used to draw me closer to Him. The thin thread I had been dangling from, unbeknownst to me, was God's hand. Without a doubt, hope is an amazingly empowering spiritual tool. It nudged my thoughts toward the right path by minimizing the worst things in my life and magnifying the best things in my life. He created in me an inner strength to overcome life's unthinkable crises. Agony became joy. Suffering brought strength. I realized that there is nothing we can do about the past. Despite how awful and painful it is, we have to leave it behind us and face the present. The question, "Why?" will never be answered. Unfortunately, it is something you must learn to accept. People often ask me how I cope with life and the death of four sons and my beloved husband. My answer is by the grace of God and the hope that each day gets better.

Problems do not always disappear; some cannot be solved, but all must be faced. We all live our lives every day with hope. I hope I get a job, I hope I lose weight, I hope the bus isn't late, and so forth. Never stop hoping; it is the foundation of a life worth living. Hope is to believe in the possibility of a positive change or outcome. Hope, without doubt, is a miraculous, empowering spiritual tool.

I know full well what it is like to have pressure in my chest because my heart was broken, and I never felt the old heart again. I suffered through mental shock and confusion to the point of thinking suicide and homicide were better options than life. The death of my children made every crisis in life pale in comparison. My heart is still broken and the temptation to cry at the slightest remembrance of my sons never goes away. My life has been altered forever. But, I stand here today as living proof that grievers can live their altered lives with an acceptable peace in their hearts.

I believe hope opened my heart and mind to believe for myself in the unseen God of the Bible; the Gospel is healing salve to my soul. I believe that my sons' spirits are whole. No more handicaps, no more operations, no more pain, and no more doctors and hospitals. Death brought an end to an overwhelmingly difficult life for my sons and husband. I have peacefully accepted that my sons transitioned from a worldly existence to an eternally wonderful and spiritual existence, and one day I will do the same. This has given me my acceptable peace. I often envision my sons in the presence of God in Heaven and me in the presence of God on Earth. We are invisible to each other, yet we are together praising the Lord. This is my joy and strength for today and hope for tomorrow.

Every day, I focus on all that is good in my life instead of the pain of the past or what I have had to let go of. I believe that I lived a remarkable and beautiful life. I spent forty-four years with a handsome man who loved me and his children. I am incredibly proud and thankful for my beautiful daughter, grandchildren, and great grandchildren. Turning seventy in 2017, I am healthy and live an abundant life. I am newly married to a wonderful man. I wonder, if I had not taken this journey, would I have the internal strength, joy of living, and zest for life that I experience today? I don't think so. Life, like a butterfly, has beautiful possibilities, but first you must transition from a caterpillar. Always know that there is still a new beginning in a crisis. Ground your hope in God and don't let your mind fool you into thinking or feeling that your circumstance is hopeless. Hope is the promise of a peaceful and an acceptable end. I dare you to hope—even if it's the smallest grain of hope. God will be with you wherever your journey takes you.

> *Hope is the promise of a peaceful and an acceptable end.*

Death is a human experience in the same manner as birth is a human experience. Both are out of man's control. We must all understand that death is complex and should never be painted with a broad brush. Who knows what someone's threshold for pain is from a loss? Death cannot be measured or evaluated by anyone but you. It is as unique to you as your fingerprint. I had several levels of suffering. I suffered through my sons' illnesses, suffered the initial pain and shock of their deaths, and suffered through the grieving, missing, and yearning to see them again. It will be an ongoing endeavor to overcome a great loss and live on. But you can.

My life was battered by the storms of life, yet as the lightning struck and the rains overflowed deep, tossing me endlessly to and fro, I kept afloat treading on the hope and faith of a caring and merciful God. And, in the end, I did not drown. He saved me.

ABOUT THE AUTHOR

Dolores Pratt Chandler is an emerging author from Pittsburgh, Pennsylvania. A mother, grandmother, corporate success, motivational speaker, and writer, she has spent a large portion of her life striving for acceptable peace and hope in the face of adversity and grief. Her positive attitude has brought her unprecedented growth and an ensuing passion for life that brings happiness to both herself and others. She lives in Pittsburgh with her husband, James.